processes used by any other successful business enterprise or organization regardless of size or type.

Thinking like a brand requires a different mindset, perspective and approach from just "business as usual." The Promise is the key to this unique approach and is absolutely fundamental for destinations to become Genuine Brands.

When a destination thinks and acts like a Genuine Brand, the entire community understands what the Promise is and how to deliver the right experience. The key for a destination to become a successful Genuine Brand is to focus on providing distinctive and relevant experiences that enrich the guest and provide lasting and memorable impressions. The destination brand comes alive through the Destination BrandScience process. A successful destination strategy goes beyond the tourism aspect; it becomes a benchmark for the entire community to become a focal point for making strategic decisions regarding growth and development. It's not the marketing "plan of the month." This is the new guide for destinations to reinvent their purpose and demonstrate their value to the community.

We developed the Destination BrandScience methodology in partnership with Duane Knapp and BrandStrategy, Inc. in 2005. Our strategy was to continue to enhance this important science for our industry's benefit and the *Global Destination BrandScience* book reflects destinations' "best practices" and brand-thought leadership. Thanks to all of our members and industry colleagues who have shared their insights for our collective benefit.

This *Global Destination BrandScience* book was developed and written to be your resource to compete more effectively and successfully by transforming your destination into a world-class brand that your stakeholders will be proud of and that guests will prefer.

Here's to your brand success!

Michael Gehrisch
President & CEO, Destination Marketing Association International

Acknowledgements

I am very thankful for the opportunity to learn from so many wonderful professionals in the destination and tourism industry, including Michael Gehrisch, Nancy Elder, Lauren Benedict, Christine Shimasaki and the entire Destination Marketing Association International team as well as Rick Antonson, Walt Judas, Paul Vallee and Sonu Purhar of Tourism Vancouver, Kevin Kane and Mary Schmitz of the Memphis Convention and Visitors Bureau, Beth Carmichael of the St. Joseph Convention & Visitors Bureau, Maura Gast of the Irving Convention and Visitors Bureau, Patsy Martin, Debbie Hamilton, Carl Molesworth, Scott Peterson and Karmen Hardy of the Port of Skagit, Peggy Campbell and Kirby Nelson from Visit Estes Park, Gretchen Hall, John Mayner and Vicki Spears of the Little Rock Convention and Visitors Bureau, Jorge Pesquera, Shirley Talbert and Kricket Marion of the Palm Beach County Convention and Visitors Bureau, Verdenia Baker of Palm Beach County, Jeffrey Vasser of the Atlantic City Convention & Visitors Authority, Joseph Marinelli of Visit Savannah, William Talbert, III of the Greater Miami Convention & Visitors Bureau, Kurt Burkhart of the Charlottesville Albemarle Convention & Visitors Bureau, James Wood and Stacy Yates Shepherd of the Louisville Convention and Visitors Bureau, Doug Traub of the Lake Havasu City Convention and Visitors Bureau, Doug Price of the Colorado Springs Convention and Visitors Bureau, Marcy Jarrett of the Enid Convention and Visitors Bureau, Misti Kerns of Santa Monica Convention and Visitors Bureau and Kelly Miller of Tampa Bay & Company.

Special thanks to each of the exceptional executives who have provided me with their valuable expertise and wisdom, including Rick Meadows, Bruce Good, Patty DeSharnais and Kelly Clark of Seabourn, Bob Cumbow of Graham & Dunn, David Evans, CHME, Bill Baker, Gerry Bruno and Paul Ouimet of InterVISTAS, Ken Uptain and Donna Braxton of Essentia Water, Inc., Sarah Blanchard of Parsons, Michael Chaffin of the Capital Hotel, Dale Carlson of Dale Carlson Marketing, Tyler McMullen of MarketVision Research, Sherrell

Reefer, Don Morgan of GMA Research, Mike Bruggeman, Greg Dunn, Ph.D., R. Blake Emery of The Boeing Company, Michael Priem of the USDM.net, Interactive Agency & Media Company, David Burke and Jim Mostad of the Breakers, Roy Assad of the Human Capital Group, Steven Ast of the Boca Raton Resort & Club, Brian McGinnis, Shaun Tucker, Marty McCormack and Jan Misner of the Alderbrook Resort and Spa, Richard Bartell of Bartell Hotels, Mike Dunn and Tom Dunn of Dunn Lumber, Professor Muthanna G. Abdul Razzaq, Ph.D., Dr. Abu Taslim Mohammad Amin, Professor Nabeel A. Jurdi, Ph.D., of the American University in the Emirates, John Mohr, Les Reardanz and Lisa Lefeber of the Port of Everett, John Jones, Tim Jewett, Sharon Schell, Steve Schell and Kelli Smith of DYKEMAN, Bruce MacCormack, Harry Levitt, Marc Williams of Williams Helde, Keefer Meranto, Phil and Melanie Multop, Tyler Ryan, Aretha Allen and Michael Lamoreux of Multop Financial, Vince Oliver, Kay Steiner, Dennis Richards and Sara Piccone of Island Hospital, Gregory S. Walsh of RWB Entertainment, Kristen Wevers of Mercy Health and David Snodgrass, Jane Kile, Danielle Brehmer and Christina Monroe of Lake Trust Credit Union, Bill Geist of Zeitgeist Consulting. I greatly appreciate Shawn Van Dyken and the entire team at Premier Graphics for their excellent printing and wonderful service.

My sincere thanks to Jackie Knapp for her design expertise, Angelita Partolan for her exceptional editing and to Dana Kirschbaum-Rodriguez of BrandStrategy, Inc. for her excellent project management and professional friendship.

Introduction

> **"***My earliest memories of my childhood involved travel and the adventures of learning something new. I was very fortunate that my mother and father enjoyed traveling.***"**

Preface

Even though our family life was modest, my parents saved money so we could travel. Driving from Michigan to my grandmother's house in Pasadena, California, on Route 66 in the 1960s was great fun. Motels with swimming pools, picnics by the side of the road and Disneyland. One summer we even rode the Super Chief train on the Santa Fe Railroad from Chicago to Los Angeles.

Travel has changed a lot since then. However, as I have traveled to hundreds of destinations around the world, one thing remains the same. Every wonderful travel experience involves someone else's kindness and service well done!

This book is dedicated to all the wonderful people in the destination, travel, tourism and hospitality industries that make visitors feel like guests and all of the talented professionals who have enhanced a destination's success by virtue of their creative strategy, design or marketing ability.

– Duane Knapp

Introduction

Global Destination BrandScience is your roadmap, a Genuine Destination Brand is your final destination. Whether you are a Destination Marketing Organization (DMO), city, county, country, Convention and Visitor's Bureau (CVB), chamber of commerce or a port authority, this book is your guide to enhancing your brand success...to develop, manage and implement a strategy to create a genuine destination brand.

This book is focused primarily on building successful destinations in the travel and tourism marketplace; however, this science can be applied to any business such as a hotel, restaurant, cruise line or attraction that wants to provide the most valued experience in their customers' minds. In fact, any business or organization that wants to become perceived as "one of a kind," rather than "one of many," can use our BrandScience principles to create competitive advantage. A Genuine Brand becomes a destination in the minds of its customers, constituents, etc. because they prefer and desire the experience that the destination provides.

A community-based organization must be equipped to embrace this mandate of defining a destination's brand. Communities that work in partnership with all of their stakeholders (attractions, hospitality businesses and infrastructure) can be brand stewards and execute a distinctive, compelling brand action plan. The Destination BrandScience methodology, which is outlined in this book, provides the disciplined process by which an organization can make a unique and meaningful contribution to the economic viability of a community beyond routine travel & tourism promotions. In short, it is this BrandPromise (Promise) commitment to create a unique destination experience that becomes the cornerstone of all strategic planning, actions and future decision making.

The Value of Science. We call this a BrandScience because it is based on a "state of knowing" and a systematic application of knowledge.

Since the introduction of the *BrandMindset®, BrandPromise®* and *Destination BrandScience™* books, I have enjoyed the pleasure of personally working with hundreds of organizations worldwide to optimize their brand success.

Science (noun). 1. The state of knowing, knowledge as distinguished from ignorance or misunderstanding. Source: Merriam Webster.

The science behind our books and methodology is proven and practical. It is based on our Promise philosophy that this science is all about creating a strategy and not just implementing tactics.

As an example, the word "branding" is widely used in relation to an organization's initiatives. Unfortunately, branding often refers to the application of a visual logo, message or promotion that is not linked to a disciplined strategy or science.

The fundamental philosophy behind Global Destination BrandScience is that it is a comprehensive and disciplined strategy for brand success. Hence, we prefer to think of this science as creating a "Strategy for a Genuine Brand" and not branding.

Destination BrandScience is focused on guiding organizations to become a "one of a kind" Genuine Brand as opposed to simply improving marketing messages. We believe that a Genuine Brand must be perceived by its target audience as distinctive.

Everyone wants the best value, however value is not just the lowest price. Consumers determine perceived value in a complex equation that includes time and feelings. The perceived value of any product or service is determined by a person's evaluation of the combination of time involved in the purchase or transaction, how they will feel about it and the cost or price paid.

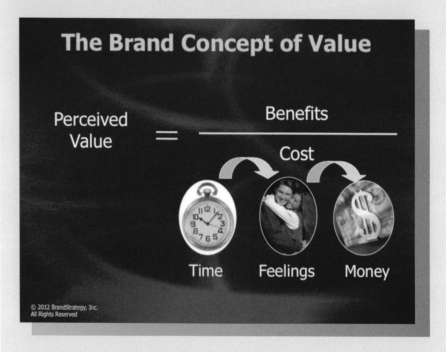

Destinations need to carefully consider how guests perceive the destination's experience in terms of the entire formula for perceived value.

Guest Mindset. Throughout this book we will be using the term "guest" to replace the traditional "visitor" reference. It's extremely important to note the reason. Our use of "guest" is based on the philosophy that a "guest" is invited and therefore has expectations. There is a strong emotional connection when someone feels like they are a valued guest.

Positive Benefits. Organizations worldwide that have embraced and implemented our strategic approach to destination brand development have seen their investment pay off in a number of measurable ways, including:

▲ Clearly defined points of distinction to distance themselves from competitors in the minds of guests.

▲ Development of a Promise that frames the destination experience from the guest's perspective as the basis for decision making and future planning.

▲ Increased revenues and profitability without the reliance on only promotion-driven marketing initiatives.

▲ Improved image as new brand initiatives revitalize a destination, replacing dated or archaic marketing practices.

▲ Culturalization of new opportunities for developing partnerships and alliances between private businesses and public organizations.

▲ Enhanced competitive positioning and market share.

▲ Increased guest financial expenditures.

▲ More engaged hospitality constituency, enhanced appreciation for the benefits of tourism and local political support.

Those communities that have accepted the challenge of creating a strategy to optimize the experience for the guest will benefit from enhanced preference, spending and other economic benefits.

Optimizing Relevance. Besides the positive benefits, there are internal goals that motivate Destination Marketing Organizations to take a pro-active leadership role in the development of a brand for their community. Now more than ever, destinations need to re-establish their relevancy in this new era of digital media. Consider these complex market dynamics:

▲ The Internet and social media have transformed the way consumers, tour operators, travel media and meeting professionals obtain information and make decisions related to destination choices as well as a variety of travel products and services.

▲ The preeminent role of established community marketing organizations as the ultimate tourism resource for communities is being seriously threatened.

▲ Destinations face many challenges, including a concentrated focus on accountability for dollars spent and a laser-like attention on Return-On-Investment (ROI).

▲ Achieving appreciation for the tourism industry and its economic benefits requires constant communications and community education.

▲ Research shows that the public supports tourism and the use of local, regional and state governments' funds to promote tourism; however, they expect a thoughtful tourism strategy.

These issues are very real; no one will argue that. But the truth is that destinations can use this leadership opportunity to establish a new relevancy with their constituents as well as revitalize and strengthen overall marketing effectiveness. Destination Marketing Organizations have a unique and important role to play in their communities' ability to succeed and thrive. However, it means refining and redefining their role. Simply put: A successful Destination Marketing Organization does for its community what the community cannot do for itself. It leads its community and stakeholders in a strategic process with the ultimate goal of creating a Genuine Destination Brand.

Five Phases to Success. As you embark on your "destination brand initiative," this book will serve as your roadmap for success. There are five phases to complete in this journey towards creating a strategy for a "Genuine Destination Brand." The phases are:

▲ **Brand Assessment**

▲ **BrandPromise**

▲ **Brand Blueprint**

▲ **Brand Culturalization**

▲ **Brand Advantage**

Chapter Outline

Chapter One – Destination BrandScience
Outlines the required Destination BrandScience mindset that is necessary for a destination to become a Genuine Brand.

Chapter Two – Destination Brand Development Roadmap
Introduces the destination brand development process.

Chapter Three – Brand Assessment
Details the process for completing a destination Brand Assessment.

Chapter Four – BrandPromise
Provides the process for developing a destination's Promise. Doing a good job is not enough – it's all about how your guests feel.

Chapter Five – Brand Blueprint

Addresses the Brand Blueprint methodology and how it guides a destination's communications plan.

Chapter Six – Brand Culturalization

Identifies the secrets for delivering a successful Promise and explains the important role that an organization's representatives play in delivering the destination's Promise.

Chapter Seven – Brand Advantage

Reveals the framework for creating destination brand alliances.

At the conclusion of each chapter, we profile a brand that we believe demonstrates an understanding of the Destination BrandScience methodology which is outlined in a Brand Insight. Each chapter also has a Thought Leadership summary which outlines key thoughts to remember as you are developing your own strategy.

Use of Specific Terminology. Please note that the following words are used to represent specific concepts to make the book a more enjoyable read.

BrandPromise	**Promise**
Brand Blueprint	**Blueprint**
Brand Assessment	**Assessment**
Genuine Destination Brand	**Genuine Brand**
Brand Doctrine	**Doctrine**

We have provided a "Brandictionary" that explains the terms listed above as well as a variety of other brand and Promise-related terms and definitions to assist in understanding the concepts behind the Destination BrandScience methodology. Please take a few minutes to review them before you read the book. Additionally, every organization should consider developing a Brandictionary guide that outlines the correct "brand-speak" for all representatives of their destination.

We have included a brand index, which lists many of the brands used as examples throughout this book. You can find that listing as well as their website address at the end of the book. You can also access this information at www.globaldestinationbrandscience.com.

Thanks to the marvels of technology, word documents can be translated into a visual which effectively highlights and presents the key ideas from a document.

We used Wordle™ (wordle.net) to translate the Global Destination BrandScience listing of chapter headings into the visual above. As the visual indicates, the key concepts in the *Global Destination BrandScience* book are presented in an easy to understand fashion.

The most prominent subjects are:

- Brand

- Destination

- Promise

- Strategy

- Genuine

- Culturalization

Any destination could use this tool to develop a visual for a newsletter, brochure or advertising copy. It provides a quick reality check for a destination's intended message.

Getting Started. There are many milestones and steps to take, but in any successful journey you will have this book to serve as your guide. Remember the first time you tried to read a map without referring to the key? It may have seemed confusing the first time, but after you learned the meanings, reading a map became second nature. Apply this same approach to your destination brand process.

The purpose of this book is quite simple – to guide your destination, community or business in the creation of a better environment for the guest, which in turn produces enhanced preference and economic benefits.

Like successful brands, great destinations are built by people who understand, embrace and follow a disciplined roadmap that outlines the essence of a truly distinctive experience from the guest's point of view.

Over the next seven chapters you will learn the keys to Destination BrandScience.

Now, let's learn how to start thinking like a Genuine Brand. Apple, Disney, Tourism Vancouver, Starbucks, Federal Express, Northwestern Mutual Life...they all do it – and you can too! ■

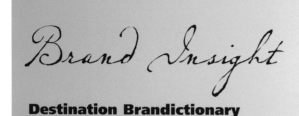

Brand Insight

Destination Brandictionary

Throughout the *Global Destination BrandScience* book, a variety of brand-related terminology is used. This Brandictionary is a ready reference to help you learn and use these keywords in your own destination brand initiative.

BrandMindset: The ability to think like a brand.

BrandPromise: (Promise) The essence of the brand's benefits – functional and emotional – that current and potential customers should expect to receive when experiencing a brand's products and services; a brand value proposition. The Promise is an internal statement.

Destination Brand Doctrine: (Doctrine) The comprehensive process or roadmap which is used by an organization to apply the Destination BrandScience and complete a brand initiative.

Brand Advantage: The result of consistent enhancing, nurturing and innovating a brand.

Brand Alliances: Utilizing partnerships with other appropriate brands to enhance an organization's brand equity.

Brand Assessment: (Assessment) An objective analysis of a brand's image and perceptions.

Brand Blueprint: 1. The disciplined action and process required to create, plan, design and build brand communications. 2. The character and structure of a brand's representations, i.e., the architecture of a brand (brand name, byline, tagline, Promise and graphic representation).

Brand Byline: A word or a short phrase of descriptive words that are part of a brand or accompany it to clearly communicate to consumers what a brand does or where to place the brand's products and services in their mind's eye (e.g., the "Visit" in Visit Estes Park or Whirlpool's brand byline: "Home Appliances").

Brand Culturalization: 1. To expose all current and future representatives to the sum total of beliefs, behaviors and ways characteristic of a particular brand. 2. To raise the level of awareness with a view toward improvement (self and organizational). 3. To live the Promise.

Brand Icon: A symbol or picture that a brand constantly associates with its brand identity to create an intended association.

Brand Name: The written identity of a destination, product, line of products or services.

Brand Tagline or Theme Lines: An expressive series of words or a short phrase used to communicate or dramatize the brand's emotional and functional benefits to consumers in an effort to influence how consumers feel about the brand, e.g., "Super, Natural" British Columbia or Nike's "Just Do It."

Brand Team: An official group of destination executives and community representatives who work together to develop a strategy for a destination brand.

Destination Brand Guide (Brand Guide): The written document which articulates the comprehensive action plan to deliver the destination's Promise in the future. The purpose is to create a paradigm shift and a "position of privilege" (sustainable competitive advantage) in order to optimize overall brand equity.

Genuine Destination Brand (Genuine Brand): The internalized sum of all impressions received by guests, influencers and stakeholders resulting in a distinctive position in their mind's eye based on perceived emotional and functional benefits.

Logo (Logotype): A graphic representation or symbol of a destination, organization, company, product, service, name, trademark, abbreviation, etc., often uniquely designed for ease of recognition.

Mind's Eye: The position in the consumer's mind that a brand occupies.

Notes

Destination BrandScience

❝Marketing organizations that create a successful Genuine Brand...focus on distinctive and relevant experiences that enrich their guests' lives and provide lasting and memorable positive impressions.❞

Communities are working together like never before to promote their common brand. It is not uncommon today for a community-wide brand initiative to include chambers of commerce, ports, economic development agencies, destination marketing organizations, city, county and state governments, airports, convention centers and other civic organizations.

While various community agencies may have somewhat different missions, they all have the same interest in creating an exceptional destination that is attractive to residents, businesses, guests, new investment and development. Jack Moneypenny, President of the Door County Visitors Bureau in Wisconsin, explains, "The bottom line is that partnerships work. It's not just true in our industry, partnerships are proving to be very effective elsewhere, but it's just that the destination marketing industry turns out to be particularly conducive to partnerships."

Our methodology has been widely utilized by hundreds of various kinds of community organizations to create successful destination strategies. The BrandScience for destinations can be applied to any community organization that truly wants to make and keep a Promise.

This chapter will focus on defining what our Destination BrandScience methodology is all about and how it applies to community brands.

As one CEO of an economic development agency said, "Tourism is the purest form of economic development."

Communities understand the importance that a brand is not just a logo or an advertising campaign; it is all about the value of making a Promise. New York City mayor Mike Bloomberg was obsessed with taking care of his residents and guests – establishing 24-hour call lines, collecting data to help develop new products and sending his executives into the field to solicit feedback directly from the community.

"Good companies listen to their customers, No. 1," he says. "Then they try to satisfy their needs, No. 2."

The Destination BrandScience process doesn't just apply to DMOs. Patsy Martin, Executive Director of the Port of Skagit (Washington State) explains, "We operate a port district (airport, marina, hiking trails and a business park). We want to provide exceptional experiences for everyone and to become preferred destinations for pilots, boaters, business owners and guests. A destination mindset leads to more good jobs for our constituents."

Gateway Development. Destinations today need to look beyond their basic tourism infrastructure to build their markets. As Paul Ouimet, Executive Vice President of InterVISTAS Consulting Inc., explains, "destinations need to be making constant improvements on a number of fronts to be successful."

Air access and transportation facilities are critical success factors for tourism, in both group and leisure markets. InterVISTAS has pioneered work in gateway development, producing action-oriented plans which improve air, ground and cruise ship capacity and service. Ouimet notes, "We have worked in several cities to bring the entire community together, business and government leaders, to address key issues affecting their competitive position. These issues often include infrastructure, service and capacity issues."

These improvements not only benefit the tourism industry but the region as a whole. The economic benefits of building a gateway city are significant. Expanded transportation can create new markets in the manufacturing, distribution and service sectors. A gateway strategy can partner perfectly with a destination's strategy for its brand.

Destination Strategy. When was the last time you were on vacation or a business trip and experienced a specific destination that was remarkable and unforgettable? Think about how you felt about your trip. What made this experience distinctive?

As the tourism marketplace becomes more competitive, it is essential that destinations continue to define themselves. Every destination has positive attributes, but these alone may not be enough to attract guests because there are other similar destinations vying for the same guests. Destinations must work to define themselves in a manner that truly offers guests a remarkable experience so that guests and tourism revenues do not go elsewhere, or they risk losing the competitive edge.

Guests have a myriad of choices when determining where to travel and each destination must ensure that it is perceived as unique and distinctive. What gives a destination a competitive edge over similarly perceived destinations or other choices? The answer is a destination's internal "Promise," the strategic mindset that makes a destination unique in the minds of guests, influencers and stakeholders.

> Destinations must come to terms with the reality that destination brand creation begins with a comprehensive strategic plan.

From a destination organization's perspective, "influencers" refers to professionals involved with arranging and managing meetings, conventions, conferences, travel-related media, and businesses that influence or direct guests to destinations for business, pleasure or both.

"Stakeholders" refers to various constituents in a community. Examples include: a destination or community organization's members (members of a destination marketing organization, convention and visitors bureau, chamber of commerce or economic development agency), tourism businesses, government agencies, residents and others who may be viewed as hosts.

A destination's strategy should address the following questions:

▲ What should our destination's distinctive Promise be?

▲ What does our destination stand for in the minds of guests, influencers and key stakeholders?

▲ What Promise experience should be communicated by our tourism representatives to our current and potential guests, influencers and other stakeholders?

▲ Are we dedicated to providing an exceptional experience for every guest?

▲ What is the consensus regarding the optimum brand image and future position for our destination?

▲ What is the most effective way to use marketing and other promotional tools to gain competitive advantage and increase our destination's success?

▲ What is the first word that we want to come to mind when prospective guests and influencers think of our destination?

▲ What brand attributes are important to our destination's varied stakeholders?

The Walt Disney Company is one of the most successful and well-respected brands in the world. Disney has developed a loyal customer base and enjoys enormous worldwide brand awareness. However, becoming a Genuine Destination Brand (Genuine Brand) requires something more complex than mere name recognition...it requires a Promise.

As Michael Priem, CEO of USDM.net, InterActive Agency and Media Company says, "Destination marketing has transformed, let alone marketing as a whole. We are in a transformative time, with never-before-available knowledge and data of our consumers. While this is powerful, we are also in a highly fragmented time where reaching and influencing that consumer arguably hasn't ever been more challenging. In the 1970's, research stated that consumers received around 500 impressions daily and the mass broadcast market was dominated by five large media networks; today research states consumers receive in the neighborhood of around 5000 impressions and there are countless media options.

While these changes have broad reaching impact on marketers in general, it also greatly impacts the destination marketing industry as well. Reaching consumers, whether on a leisure perspective or group basis, now means that there are more options, so how do we choose? Where does 'brand' influence this and how do we build a 'brand,' especially when reaching a target that at moments appears to be moving? Advertising and marketing have long stated that 'impressions create impressions,' but now impressions are also clicks and performance metrics, not just ratings and market share. Marketers have to understand not just how to build 'brand equity' but also the marriage of technology and research in order to drive performance today."

Michael further comments that "whether it's at the conceptual level of building the brand, or execution of a campaign, the anthropology of the audience must be understood. With anthropology now front and center, marketers and advertisers need to examine how brands communicate. The public is bombarded with social media and the entire digital shift. We must, however, focus on how we MESSAGE our audience and it is important to recognize that worldwide, we are in a trust deficit."

What should a destination brand be about? Successful brands are built on a Promise.

Cities are more than a mere collection of buildings, just as places are more than mountains, trees or beaches. Cities and places are about people's aspirations, their hopes and dreams and – most important – their memories. This is why countries, regions and cities are places of imagination. People want to go and experience firsthand that which they have heard, seen or read about. A successful brand captures people's imagination.

A brand is not just a slogan, and a slogan is not a strategy! The easiest way to understand the concept of a destination brand is to define what it is not about. A strategy is not just:

▲ Introducing high technology digital communications.

▲ Launching an extensive or expensive ad campaign.

▲ Creating a glitzy new logo, design scheme, catchy slogan or tagline.

▲ Posting pretty pictures and matching stationery.

▲ Initiating a public relations campaign.

▲ Distributing glossy brochures.

▲ Creating a trade show booth.

In fact, many academics define brand management as a "positioning" exercise with no attention paid to the Promise or experience. Much of what is called "branding" today is, in fact, nothing more than promotion and hype.

A Genuine Brand is much deeper and richer than the artificial constructs that are so commonly passed off as "branding." While all of the marketing elements described above help deliver and define the brand, they are not the definition of the brand. More importantly, they are not the foundation for a Genuine Brand initiative.

Far too often, destinations get caught up in the visual trappings of the brand process, without a clear picture of the desired result from the guest's perspective. Consultants and advertising agencies may profess to understand the process, but so often new branding campaigns generally produce nothing more than expensive new messaging, advertising or logos. Typically, destinations and their constituents are too focused on marketing a promotion message. Before an advertising or creative agency is called in, a destination must come to terms with the reality that a destination strategy begins with a comprehensive Brand Assessment.

BrandMindset. Destinations, by definition, are comprised of many interrelated parts. There are perhaps thousands of independent businesses and individuals that, by virtue of their location and relationship within the destination, make up the destination brand product or experience. Nearly all of these elements are made up of people who are not necessarily professionally or organizationally connected. They sell a variety of products and services. They may have various degrees of business sophistication, loyalty and commitment to the community or even to the local tourism industry.

With so many different parts throughout a destination that are seemingly unconnected and disparate, how is it possible to create a cohesive destination brand? Of course it can and must, to survive and thrive in today's ultra-competitive global marketplace. While it can be challenging, a destination can certainly execute a successful brand initiative by marshalling its forces and unifying its key constituents and stakeholders within the destination community. But first, it needs to understand and embrace the mindset of becoming a Genuine Brand.

It's not unlike a hotel brand like Hampton Inn. Most Hampton Inns are owned by franchisees, so how can Hampton Inns be so exceptional? The answer...they all have the same internal Promise.

Genuine Brand Defined. There are three fundamental traits that differentiate a Genuine Brand in consumers' minds. They are:

▲ The internalized sum of their impressions

▲ A distinctive position in their mind's eye

▲ Perceived functional and emotional benefits

By definition, a Genuine Brand is the internalized sum of all impressions received by guests and influencers, resulting in a distinctive position in their mind's eye based on perceived emotional and functional benefits.

> A key objective of a Genuine Brand should be to add value to people's lives. A Genuine Brand is about benefiting the consumer and the more distinctive a brand is, the easier it is to communicate effectively to the consumer.

Genuine Brands clearly need to be different from similar products and become perceived as more relevant to consumer's lives. In today's global marketplace, companies with successful brands understand what "business" they are in. They know that first and foremost, they are in the service business. Exceeding customer expectations will be the defining factor in distinguishing their brand from the competition in the eyes and minds of the consumers. The primary goal of any brand initiative should always be to create preference in the minds of the target audience, not just awareness.

A Genuine Brand adds value to people's lives.

It has long been believed that the way to build a Genuine Brand was to follow the F.R.E.D model:

▲ Familiarity

▲ Relevance

▲ Esteem

▲ Differentiation

Organizations often thought that the most important part of F.R.E.D was to make a consumer familiar with a brand's product and service offering. While no one would argue that awareness is important in the life of a brand, that theory is now considered outdated. This theory implied that if your product was well known through advertising, it was considered a "brand." In today's world, consumers are over-saturated with thousands of messages every day and choices on everything, from digital cameras to coffees. Hence, the critical issue for a destination is to distinguish its experience and reputation in ways that guests find relevant, meaningful and valuable.

Starbucks, one of the greatest brands to emerge in the last 25 years, did not build its "third place" brand by focusing on an expensive national advertising campaign. For years, Starbucks spent more energy on training than advertising. For a brand to be noticed and eventually chosen, it must be effective at communicating its unique attributes in a wide variety of applications. Building a successful brand can be done without an extensive or expensive advertising campaign. Great brands, such as Starbucks, were not built on advertising: they were built around a Promise. So too were Tiffany and Zappos. Why do some succeed where other seemingly highly recognized brands fail?...It's all about the Promise.

With an overabundance of specialty magazines, cable television channels, radio stations and outdoor advertising opportunities, the consumer is bombarded with literally thousands of promotion and advertising messages every day. Advertising agencies acknowledge the challenge of finding "breakthrough" concepts that can engage the consumer.

Consumers Want Authentic Experiences. Today's consumers are savvy. They are more educated and scrutinize advertising through a different set of filters than they did just a few years ago. They are not necessarily any less susceptible to advertising; however, they are just inundated with more of it.

> The key for marketing organizations to become a successful Genuine Brand is to focus on distinctive and relevant experiences that enrich the guest and provide lasting and memorable impressions.

What does this mean to the destination industry? Traveler research indicates that guests are actively seeking out "authentic" experiences, be it a culinary retreat, outdoor adventure or surf camps. Even theme parks can be "authentic" if they offer distinctive experiences such as man-made fantasies, genuine adventure or real family entertainment. The ever-increasingly sophisticated guest understands that advertising alone can't possibly tell the whole story.

Breaking the Promise. Guests are engaged on many different levels. They are turned off by products positioned one way when the reality of the experience is something entirely different. For example:

▲ A "relaxing" resort that, in truth, has noisy traffic congestion

▲ An "exciting" downtown that actually closes up after 5 p.m.

▲ A "family-oriented" hotel that has no family programs

In many cases, the pictures used in vacation brochures to promote a destination may not even be from that location. But to the guests, they are real. Destinations must be careful not to create a set of expectations through marketing that may not be fulfilled for the guest.

There are many communities with beaches, lakes, mountains and museums. All have hotels, restaurants and attractions. As communities continue to develop their infrastructure, a "sea of sameness" is creeping into the travel experience that is similar to what is now plaguing retail in general. Hotels look the same in different cities, chain restaurants pop up internationally and even theme parks offer the same attractions in different parts of the world. Destinations must deal with this reality and be honest about their uniqueness.

Becoming a Successful Genuine Brand. There are currently hundreds of major Destination Marketing Organizations in the world. All of them are working to position their communities to gain a favorable market share of guests' dollars. While many concentrate a vast amount of their energies and resources to create interesting marketing programs, a marketing program alone is not enough to attain, or better, earn the privilege of Genuine Brand status. Destinations must transcend the usual marketing routine and focus on that which is meaningful to guests if they are to grow their business. The key for marketing organizations to become a successful Genuine Brand, is to focus on distinctive and relevant experiences that enrich the guest and provide lasting and memorable impressions. So how does a destination go about this?

The Destination Action Plan. Our process for developing a Genuine Brand is called the Destination Brand Doctrine (Doctrine) and it is a comprehensive action plan to:

▲ Define a destination's essence: its Promise commitment.

▲ Create a perceived brand paradigm shift and become distinctive in the guest's mind apart from other or similar destinations.

▲ Optimize economic opportunity and create a sustainable competitive advantage.

Follow the Doctrine to Create a Distinctive Brand Experience. This Doctrine, below, is based on our award winning books, *The BrandMindset* and *The BrandPromise*, published by McGraw-Hill. Hundreds of destinations, as well as travel and hospitality corporations worldwide have utilized the Global Destination BrandScience methodology described in this book. The overall result of this Doctrine is to provide destinations with the expertise to create a strong, competitive position that will distinguish it from its competition.

It should be noted that destinations address a variety of market segments including convention sales, tourism trade and leisure guests. The development of this brand leadership should be universal in scope

HOW TO CREATE A GENUINE DESTINATION BRAND EXPERIENCE

1. Brand Assessment — — → Define the community's essence and experiential commitment.

2. BrandPromise — — → Create a unique Promise and paradigm shift.

3. Brand Blueprint — — → Become distinctive in guests' minds apart from other destinations.

4. Brand Culturalization — — → Think like a brand; live the destination's Promise.

5. Brand Advantage — — → Optimize economic opportunity; form alliances to enhance brand equity.

and cross all market segments. This means that the strategy for a destination brand and the development of a Promise will be uniform. While the tactics for the delivery of the Promise may be different for the meeting planner than for the leisure guest, the Promise will be the same for all activities.

The result of this process will also help destinations rethink, re-energize and restructure their marketing plans. The traditional approach has been to create a budget and then a marketing plan, which in turn drives the organization's activities. On the contrary, in a Genuine Brand environment, it is essential that the overall strategy for a destination brand initiative drive all of an organization's activities, as well as the marketing plan and then the budget, not the other way around.

A destination's key leadership must embrace and feel deeply that the Doctrine holds great power to influence the direction of the organization and gain greater guest market share. This Doctrine cannot be relegated to the marketing or advertising departments. The program must have the full authority of the destination executive team, board of directors and the leaders of other key community organizations in order to succeed.

A destination brand initiative can literally revolutionize the purpose and direction of a destination if it is well thought out with significant stakeholder and constituent consensus. The initiative can give meaningful shape to programming and creative decisions that are a part of a destination's daily existence by clarifying the destination's unique value proposition.

According to Gretchen Hall, President and CEO of the Little Rock Convention and Visitors Bureau, "We have a long history of working with BrandStrategy, Inc. What we discovered during our Brand Assessment was that our genuine and sincere people are a huge part of what sets us apart as a destination. That is particularly exciting for us as the destination marketing organization because we know it will take all facets of the destination to support and deliver our new Promise. We see this process as a roadmap and methodology to unify our stakeholders, and community as a whole, and move the destination forward with a focus on the customer experience. We believe in the Destination BrandScience process and know that it will be valuable for all of our hospitality staff and stakeholders in our efforts to coalesce one strategy, one Promise and deliver one exceptional Little Rock experience."

Adventure On. Before a destination begins this adventure, it is wise to understand the effort involved and the commitment from all staff to make the strategic approach to destination brand development the foundation and focus of the destination's existence. Everyone, including the destination's board and committee leadership, will need to be involved and support the development of a Genuine Brand with resources and staff time.

While brand leadership is perhaps one of the most important roles a destination organization can play in the life of its community, the process demands:

▲ An "inclusive" community partnership philosophy.

▲ Strong community leadership.

▲ Strict discipline to follow the science.

▲ Objectivity as well as an open mindset.

▲ Willingness to ask tough questions about themselves and their communities.

▲ The ability to accept honest answers in return, both the good and the not so good.

▲ Recognition that it is not the place for political correctness or community pandering.

Experience indicates that all too often an internal approach falls short in four areas:

▲ Lack of objectivity

▲ Difficulty in gaining a real consensus

▲ Absence of significant results

▲ Hype rather than substance

Successful brands are not created overnight or accomplished by an elite group of individuals. Just as cities are more than buildings, streets and businesses, brands are the result of the people who interact with them.

Brand Investment. Destinations need to consider setting aside the appropriate resources for a brand initiative project, including contracting with a third party expert or "guide," who fully understands and embraces the Destination Brand Science. For smaller destinations, their strategy "guide" may be a board member or community leader who can lead the process in partnership with the destination executive team. This individual is often critical to the success of the program since the destination and its community stakeholders will often have to address sensitive and even painful issues related to the destination, its community and vital stakeholders. As Marcy Jarrett, Director of the Enid Convention & Visitors Bureau says, "You don't have to be a large destination with a big budget to create a successful strategy for your brand."

A brand is the yardstick by which guests measure their destination experience. Be genuine!

The suggested amount to budget for this process will vary widely, depending upon the need for third-party research, the experience and expertise of the facilitator and the scope of involvement. It is also recommended to budget for the publication of the Brand Guide report, which summarizes the destination's strategy, outlines its Promise and includes the graphic representation for the destination brand. This important document gives key stakeholders and the board a clear understanding of the destination's strategy and how board members and community leaders can support the program. It is also important to budget for a community Promise Training Guide and training sessions so that everyone knows how to deliver the destination's Promise.

Once a destination – and the community it represents – fully commits to the Doctrine process and determines its resources and contractor costs, it is ready to begin the journey. ■

Brand Insight

Bourbon Country Communities Working Together to Build a Brand

The "Bourbon Country" brand has taken nearly 200 years to evolve. As America's only native spirit, bourbon whiskey has been produced in Kentucky since the farmer-distillers of the late 1700's settled in the area bringing their stills in tow from the north and their European distillation recipes from "the old country." With an abundance of corn and limestone-fed water, it was just a matter of time before those barrels from the original "Bourbon County" shipped downriver to eager consumers in New Orleans evolved to simply "bourbon." Now producing 95% of the world's supply of this signature spirit across several counties, Kentucky simply IS Bourbon Country.

The marketing of this region to potential guests has not been 200 years in the making. To the contrary, even though bourbon was regarded as one of the state's signature exports, tourism to the region for the purpose of a bourbon "experience" was not officially promoted as such until the 1990's. The city of Bardstown was the first destination to distinctly promote bourbon tourism by defining the town as the "Bourbon Capital of the World" for the production that takes place in the county and the founding of a Kentucky Bourbon Festival to support that claim in 1992. In 1999, several distilleries that were members of the Kentucky Distillers' Association worked to form a "trail" to promote visitation to their production facilities. The Kentucky Bourbon Trail® launched with seven distilleries and a limited budget to market the attraction.

The Louisville Convention & Visitors Bureau (LCVB) began working with the Kentucky Distillers' Association in 2004 to explore marketing distillery tours to potential guests coming to Kentucky through Louisville. A new Visitors Center opened in Louisville in early 2007 with the Kentucky Bourbon Trail® as a featured exhibit. Louisville also positioned itself as the Gateway to Bourbon Country.

Seeing the interest in bourbon production and culture as a tourism draw, Louisville begin researching how best to draw on the city's unique distilling heritage to attract guests even without a public distillery tour on the trail. The LCVB hired a local agency, Bandy Carroll Hellige, to do a market study of interest in bourbon tourism and test some potential names to define the region. "Bourbon Country" was born out of this research and testing. It was not a brand that had to be created. It was the essence of the culture in Kentucky. Many distillers, Kentucky natives and writers had been using the term in conversation and in print for over 100 years and it seemed a logical comparison to "Wine Country" which had served as a model for the vision of marketing the region collectively.

A logo, color scheme and font were selected for the new "Bourbon Country" brand in late 2006 before the Visitor Center opened. 15,000 branded rack cards were printed in order to be ready for guests and the marketing campaign was launched in 2007. This included print advertising and a broadcast commercial aired locally and regionally. As momentum for the campaign grew, the LCVB sought other destination marketing organizations that had distilleries in their area to form a strategic marketing partnership. The cities of Bardstown, Frankfort, Shepherdsville, Lebanon, Versailles and Lawrenceburg joined Louisville and the Kentucky Distillers Association to provide marketing support for growing the brand. The LCVB funded all marketing efforts of Bourbon Country at that time.

The purpose of the marketing campaign, beyond generating visitation, is to "romance" the entire region that encompasses not only the bourbon production, but the experience, culture and heritage that surrounds it. Many know the Napa and Sonoma Valleys in California as "Wine Country," though Italy, France and even Virginia and Oregon might take issue. There is only ONE Bourbon Country. The goal is to establish an entire lifestyle that can be associated with this region...so that it becomes more than just a tour of distilleries.

Since 2007, more than $3 million has been invested in a comprehensive campaign to build the brand. A brand standards manual has been developed. From traditional broadcast and print media to social networking, event marketing, public relations, website and digital media, out-of-home billboards and an official magazine, the Bourbon Country brand has resonated with regional, national and international audiences. Interstate hotels utilized the brand in its in-house restaurant promotion "Flavors from Bourbon Country." Alltech has adopted the advertising phrase for one of its beer promotions "the official beer of Bourbon Country" and a new country band has formed taking the name the Bourbon Country Band. Locally in Louisville, they have created the Urban Bourbon Trail around downtown Louisville. Guests can visit dozens of hotels, restaurants and bars where they can enjoy a "spirits experience" and taste 50-150 bourbons and learn all about Louisville's bourbon heritage.

In the fall of 2011, tourism officials worked to evolve from the occasional committee meeting to forming an official alliance to market the destination in a unified effort. The Louisville Convention & Visitors Bureau, owner of the Bourbon Country brand, issued licensing agreements to its neighboring DMO partners. Now the region is working collaboratively in promoting the Bourbon Country brand individually and collectively. In September 2012, the Bourbon Country region launched the www.bourboncountry.com website as well as a Bourbon Country Visitors Guide. This regional coalition of tourism agencies in the state now works to cooperatively market and fund Bourbon Country as a leading incentive to travel to Kentucky.

❏ Is your community prepared to commit to a guest mindset, i.e., providing distinctive and relevant experiences that enrich guests and provide lasting and memorable impressions?

❏ Gain agreement that the destination strategy for your brand will drive all of the destination's activities, including the marketing plan and budget.

❏ Gain commitment from the destination leadership team and board, as appropriate, before you embark on a destination brand initiative.

❏ Involve destination staff, board members and committee leadership in the process and development of a Genuine Brand.

❏ As appropriate, budget resources to contract with a third party expert who understands and embraces the Destination BrandScience process, a third party research company to provide guest and community research and for the publication of the Doctrine report which summarizes the strategy for your board and community leaders.

Chapter Two

Destination Brand
Development Roadmap

Developing a strategy is the primary deliverable in the Destination BrandScience process. As such, a destination should understand that this process, although at times creative in nature, is a disciplined, intellectual exercise that involves visionary leadership.

The Doctrine Is Your Roadmap. The disciplined methodology for developing a Genuine Brand is the process outlined in the chart below. This process results in a written roadmap that includes five primary action steps:

1. Assessing the destination's current situation, brand perceptions and future prospects.

2. Developing a Promise for the destination.

3. Creating the Brand Blueprint for communications.

4. Finalizing a Brand Culturalization plan that can be employed by the destination and the community as a whole to deliver the Promise.

5. Establishing Brand Advantages.

The fundamental philosophy of the Doctrine is that everything relating to the Doctrine must include guests', influencers' and stakeholders' perspectives and represent an objective viewpoint. Influencers include

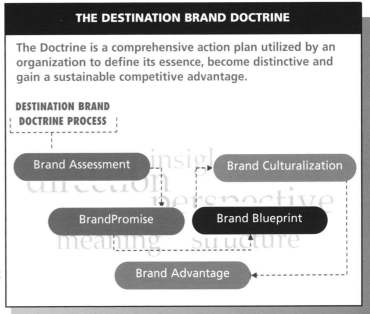

THE DESTINATION BRAND DOCTRINE

The Doctrine is a comprehensive action plan utilized by an organization to define its essence, become distinctive and gain a sustainable competitive advantage.

DESTINATION BRAND DOCTRINE PROCESS

- Brand Assessment
- Brand Culturalization
- BrandPromise
- Brand Blueprint
- Brand Advantage

meeting professionals, destination members, tour operators, etc. Stakeholders are community leaders and constituents. In order for the destination brand to succeed, it must include the benefits of many perspectives, especially the appropriate guest and consumer insights. All too often destination boards, which by their very nature are loyal and protective of their destination, "cover up" the flaws of their community by benignly ignoring them or choosing to dwell only on the positives. At the outset of this process, staff and the destination leadership have to put aside preconceived perceptions, both good and bad, and see the destination from the guest's perspective. The value of the Doctrine is that it forces objectivity and discipline as well as providing a structured roadmap for all to follow.

Destination Brand Initiative Leadership. It is important to note that the process will not succeed if the DMO's chief executive officer and the board are not active and engaged partners in the effort. With so many responsibilities, it is easy for a destination's leadership to view a brand initiative as just the next marketing plan. Instead, view your brand initiative as a chance to demonstrate relevancy and provide enhanced value as well as a high-profile community service. The board has an important role to fill and will have to make sure that the development of the destination brand becomes one of its most important initiatives in the destination's program of work. They also may need to be educated on how the brand will benefit their respective businesses and create increased revenues and profits, and how they will share responsibility for the implementation of the Promise once it is finalized.

A brand team should be developed with fewer than 10 members including community leaders, DMO and tourism business executives, representing a cross-section of the organization's operations. The members of the brand team should be the "best and brightest" of a destination's representatives. They should be varied in position, level and area of responsibility, and they should include executive, front-line, marketing and so on. It typically can take six to twelve months to complete a brand initiative, depending on the size and complexity of a destination.

For destinations with staff who possess little formal training in marketing or brand management, the Doctrine can provide a formal method to begin the effort that is relevant, fact-based and easy to use for the development of a Genuine Brand.

Why use the word Doctrine? Simply put, a Doctrine is something to be taken seriously. It is based on policy, principles and a system of teachings. A Genuine Brand requires a serious Doctrine based on specific principles that a destination believes are fundamental and which, in turn, determine the key policies and actions necessary for transforming a destination into a Genuine Brand.

Step 1: Brand Assessment. After a destination agrees to create a Genuine Brand using the Doctrine process and submits to the rigorous nature of the work involved, the first step in the process is to conduct a thorough assessment of the brand's current position. This is an independent "situation analysis" of the marketplace including:

▲ Guests

▲ Community

▲ Meeting professionals

▲ Travel media and other customers

▲ Relevant economic and industry conditions supported by demographic and psychographic trends

> Successful destination brands are entirely focused on the experience they intend to deliver and on the emotional and functional benefits, which result in delighting guests and in turn, create enormous competitive advantages.

The city, the chamber of commerce or county economic development department or other business-marketing agencies can assist getting the latest information. In fact, it is often advisable to make such groups an active and engaged partner in the Doctrine process, so that they have a meaningful role in developing the program and can be active participants when it comes to the Brand Culturalization phase.

Step 2: The Promise. Once the Assessment is completed, the most important aspect of the Doctrine is the Promise or value proposition. The Promise is defined as: the essence of the benefits (both functional and emotional) that current and potential guests can expect to receive from experiencing the destination. The Promise incorporates the guest's point of view and is intended to reflect the heart, soul and spirit of the brand. It is intended to serve as an **internal** directive related to how a destination wants its guests to feel. It is not the advertising message, although it must drive all of the destination's activities as well as marketing, promotions, etc.

Promising an Experience. Community leaders should follow a strategy that results in their destination being perceived as distinctive from other choices, being more relevant to their guests and influencers, and offering superior perceived value.

In today's challenging environment, Destination Marketing Organizations are expected to provide brand leadership for their members, not just promote a destination. A successful destination must think like a Genuine Brand from two perspectives – as a destination and as a convention and visitors bureau or destination marketing organization – and this requires a mindset, perspective and strategy that is different from business as usual. Successful destinations need to be perceived as distinctive and need to make a Promise to their guests that delivers emotional and functional benefits. The Destination Marketing Association International created a directional Promise for its member organizations.

Destination Marketing Organizations are positioned to be brand stewards for destinations. Destinations can distinguish themselves...develop a Promise, increase revenues and profits, and create a better environment for the guest, which results in unique destination experiences that become the cornerstone for all strategic planning, actions and future decision making.

Official Destination Marketing Organization Promise Concept

"We are the guest's and meeting professional's trusted partner – the heart, soul and energy of our destination. We drive economic success and enhance the quality of life in our communities. Our communities appreciate our contribution: The better the destination, the better the experience."

When a destination thinks and acts like a Genuine Brand, the entire community understands what the Promise is and how it can deliver the right experience. Leading destination organizations that deliver on their Promise to their members and guests will benefit from enhanced member satisfaction and guest demand that provide profitable pricing opportunities for the business community, an increase in pride and tax benefits, as well as the power of a positive experience. The key for a destination to become a successful Genuine Brand is to focus on providing distinctive and relevant experiences that enrich the guest and provide lasting and memorable impressions.

A great brand is more than just name recognition. It is an emotional attachment to the product and an expectation of service or quality that consistently leaves the consumer feeling delighted regardless of the price paid. Genuine Brands are cultivated and developed, not organically grown. In the case of destinations, in order for them to compete, they must be more than simply a place to visit. They must produce an emotional connection with the consumer that transcends just products and services, such as attractions or things do, or price points. There is nothing like visiting a destination that provides a unique, exceptional experience.

Thinking like a brand requires a different mindset, and the Promise is the key to this unique approach. It is absolutely fundamental to creating, developing or enhancing a new or existing Genuine Brand.

Meaningful Distinction Inspires Confidence in the Purchase Decision. The key for destinations is to learn how they can distinguish themselves from their competition. With the growth of international theme parks, restaurants and shopping centers, a bland sameness is creeping into the American travel experience. Many cities are looking like others just a few miles away. A successful Promise must express the unique benefits that a destination brand offers to its guests. Even a city with a distinctive destination product will have difficulty if the guest's experience is not a good one. Part of Disney's theme park success is based on the fact that each "cast member" is trained to "put on a show" when they are "on stage" in the park – even the street sweepers. Employee training and the focus on the guest experience is just as important to the Walt Disney Company as developing thrilling new attractions.

The Promise is the most critical component of the brand.

Wording of the Promise should not be taken lightly. A destination's commitment and dedication to offering superior value, meaningful differentiation and executional excellence should be clearly expressed. The level to which a destination brand and its stakeholders "live" its Promise, is measured from their guests' perspectives. Guests will determine whether or not a destination has reached Genuine Brand status.

Step 3: Brand Blueprint. After the Promise has been finalized, the destination brand's architecture, or Blueprint, can be developed. The Blueprint outlines the various types of messages that will be used to communicate the Promise. These include:

▲ The name

▲ Brand representation (logo)

▲ Byline

▲ Tagline

▲ Story

The purpose of the Blueprint is to call out or set forth the types of messages to be used to communicate the brand's essence, not dictate the messages themselves. This is where, once the strategy has been developed and consensus reached among decision-makers and key stakeholders, creative professionals enter the process as partners to help craft the actual campaign themes and statements consistent with the brand's Promise.

A Slogan is Not a Strategy. A Genuine Brand is not simply the result of a catchy slogan or advertising message. It seems as though every couple of days, some destination is announcing its new slogan. The following headlines tell the story:

"Need a Fast Buck? Come Up with a Slogan"

"County Launches New Advertising"

"New State Tourism Tagline Unveiled"

"City Reveals Stylish New Tagline"

Unfortunately, it seems that slogans come and go all too often. Millions of dollars are wasted on slogans and advertising taglines that don't work. Of course, it's easy to second-guess any advertising slogan or campaign.

Situations like this illuminate several important issues. For example, a leading computer manufacturer would never knowingly put the Intel logo on a computer without the Intel chip actually being inside. "Intel Inside" delivers a Promise of performance and hopefully an exceptional experience for the consumer.

Destinations should be the same. Long before anyone even thinks about a slogan or an advertising campaign, a destination should create a comprehensive strategy that includes a Promise. A destination's Promise must be linked to an experience that has been well thought out and one that is focused on how a destination wants its guests to feel.

A destination and its entire community including government, residents and tourism industry employees (taxi drivers, public safety, police, fire, restaurant, hotel and convention center) must put a plan in motion to deliver that desired Promise and experience. Everyone involved in the guest's experience is responsible for how a destination's guests feel and their perceptions. This is not to say that a well-conceived slogan cannot contribute to a destination's success. However, a slogan or advertising theme should be based on the desired Promise.

Step 4: Brand Culturalization. The next step in the destination brand process actually helps ensure that the destination brand comes to life and endures for many years by preparing a written action plan (Brand Guide) that outlines a destination's strategy. The Brand Guide, often overlooked or short-changed during development, is an integral, critically important aspect of the entire process bringing together the key components of the destination brand including the brand's Promise, brand principles and culturalization plan.

The written Brand Guide does more than merely validate the importance of the destination brand process. It does much more:

▲ It serves the destination as the source document providing details of the research findings and the rationale behind the Promise.

▲ When a destination completes the Doctrine process, it will need to communicate its new Promise and all of the brand components to its members, key stakeholders and community leaders.

▲ The written Brand Guide is an excellent "leave behind" that provides legitimacy to a brand initiative and promotes the appropriate "buy in" from organizations and stakeholders who will need to incorporate the program into their own businesses.

▲ This document should be updated annually before the marketing plan and the budget process or at least every two years as appropriate to reflect the consistent nurturing and innovation of the brand.

Step 5: Brand Advantage. The Brand Advantage process is based on the philosophy that building a Genuine Brand is not a six month or a "once and done" project but rather a long term process. Genuine Brands require constant disciplined innovation and improvement. Brand Advantage is all about a continuous program of building and enhancing perceived distinctiveness with brand alliances and other brand enhancement strategies.

Being Distinctive is a Requirement – Not an Option.

As discussed earlier, it is important for a destination brand to be distinctive. This is not an optional idea. It is simply not possible to have a Genuine Brand without achieving the perception of being distinctive to the guest. The purpose of the Doctrine process is to identify, develop, maintain or enhance the brand's unique characteristics from which distinctive perceptions of the destination occur in the minds of guests. Destination distinctiveness can be defined in the following manner:

The guest must acknowledge the distinctiveness of the destination intellectually as well as feel it, providing a strong emotional connection with the destination.

▲ Separateness – not being like other destinations

▲ Difference in nature or quality

▲ Prominence – clear to the senses

▲ Special quality, style or attractiveness

▲ Excellence – superiority – prominence

▲ Conspicuousness – eminence

It's clear that the word distinctive is intended to possess a positive connotation. Note the consistency of such descriptors as prominent, attractiveness and excellence. This is consistent with the concept that a brand should be aspirational and invoke a positive feeling, as well as a sense of pride. The Doctrine process should be focused on identifying, communicating and delivering a destination brand's distinctive characteristics that are important to its stakeholders and especially the guest.

Being Distinctive Enhances Your Compelling Selling

Proposition. It is absolutely critical for a destination brand to identify its current or desired distinctive characteristics in its Promise. Some destinations may not understand that being distinctive is critical to defining their selling proposition or value proposition. Although destinations sometimes think they have a compelling selling proposition, in reality they often fail to understand their destination's true character. As a result, communities are often painted with a blandness that fails to motivate guests. Clever ad campaigns or slogans cannot cover up an uninspiring destination that has not discovered its true essence.

View your strategy for your brand as a chance for the destination to demonstrate relevancy and provide enhanced value.

In many cases, a destination:

▲ Doesn't understand the need to be distinctive.

▲ Has difficulty in identifying its distinctive characteristics.

▲ Has difficulty in creating a perception of distinctiveness.

▲ Fails to note the changing character of its communities and the impact on guest experiences.

▲ Chooses to communicate the wrong characteristics, which may not be beneficial, valued or desired by guests.

It is important to note that it is not enough to only be distinctive, the target audience must perceive the brand's attributes to be truly beneficial and distinctive in their mind's eye. For example:

▲ Hosting the Olympics provides destinations with the opportunity to present their experience on the worldwide stage.

▲ Las Vegas has finally acknowledged that it is an adult fantasy destination after attempting to brand itself as a family entertainment market.

▲ Australia has become perceived as a beautiful, adventurous and one-of-a-kind destination thanks to Crocodile Dundee. It should be noted that even these movies were part of a strategy to distinguish Australia.

If a destination decides that it truly wishes to become a Genuine Brand, there are virtually an unlimited number of options. The secret is to have the desire and passion to become perceived as a real distinctive brand and select or develop distinctive attributes that guests will value. It takes candor, honesty and an ability to step into the guest's shoes to see the destination from his and her point of view. ■

Brand Initiative Success Check List

From years of hands-on experience working with tourism destination organizations and hundreds of brands, seven qualities emerge as inherent among successful Genuine Brands.

1. Required buy-in. From the outset, leadership and key stakeholders have to believe wholeheartedly and enthusiastically in the approach, or the destination brand will fall short of its anticipated goals.

2. It's all about the strategy. To become a distinctive, one-of-a-kind destination brand that wins the hearts and minds of guests requires an integrated strategy for brand development. Brands are more than names, symbols or slogans. A Genuine Brand is "the internalized sum of all impressions received by guests and prospective guests, resulting in a distinctive position in their 'mind's eye' based on perceived emotional and functional behavior." Advertising and promotion are important, but only after a distinctive Promise is developed. Remember, from the guests' perspective, a destination brand is all about the experience.

3. Principles first. Establish a set of brand values and principles to guide behavior and decision-making.

4. Stand out to stand apart. A destination's strategy for its brand must be built on a set of attributes and factors that distinguish it from competitors in the minds and perspectives of guests, influencers and stakeholders.

5. Brand evangelists wanted. To ensure total commitment and community support, everyone throughout the organizations (from the very top to the very bottom) becomes an evangelist for the brand. No one person alone can champion the cause. It takes a team to ensure that all messages are aligned with the Promise.

6. Commitment and discipline. Staying true to the road map by following the designated course of action and messages is the path to attaining destination brand goals.

7. Deliver on the Promise. A Genuine Brand is a pact with guests. Successful brands keep their commitments with guests and enthusiastically deliver on the Promise.

Genuine Brand

"The internalized sum of all impressions received by guests and influencers resulting in a distinctive position in their mind's eye based on perceived emotional and functional benefits."

Duane Knapp

Guests must be able to trust the destination brand to deliver a distinctive, pleasurable and memorable experience each and every time they visit.

Before you can be heard, you have to know who your audience is and what they think about your destination.

39

Brand Insight

Modesty, Acknowledgement and Leadership in Palm Beach County

Introduction. It all starts with a little modesty. The notion that there is always a need to learn more, study, analyze and question how a destination is perceived by the guests; the feelings evoked when the name comes up in conversation, a news article or advertisement.

The evolution of a Genuine Brand should begin with a strategy ensuring the successful completion of the Destination BrandScience process. DMO representatives need to understand that the process is a disciplined intellectual exercise that involves visionary leadership.

This is how it all started in Palm Beach County, Florida.

Modesty and Acknowledgement. When the search for a new CEO for the Palm Beach County Convention & Visitors Bureau (PBC CVB) took place, the candidate was asked the usual question – what would be one of the first projects you would undertake if chosen for this position? The answer came immediately and without hesitation: a destination Brand Assessment.

The candidate explained how he, a fairly well travelled tourism executive did not have a clear picture of Palm Beach County as a destination before being contacted by the search company. He had driven through the area a few years prior, but could not picture where or what would be considered the epicenter of tourism activity. It was not clear if the destination was comprised of several tourism intensive urban centers or a disconnected variety of luxury resorts along the Atlantic coast.

As the candidate, Jorge Pesquera, who was subsequently hired as President and CEO of the Palm Beach County Convention & Visitors Bureau noted, "If someone like me is unclear about the destination, imagine the confusing impressions among the less travelled consumer market."

This was the seed of modesty: acknowledging the need to know more about how your destination is perceived in order to chart a roadmap toward becoming a "one of a kind" destination.

Leadership...Gaining Allies and Rallying Support. By the next summer, the PBC CVB's Board of Directors had blessed, in principle, the investment required to conduct a professionally facilitated Brand Assessment. The board was comprised of key leaders from the local hospitality community, including general managers and top marketing executives of world renowned hotels including the Boca Raton Resort & Spa and The Breakers in Palm Beach.

They shared Pesquera's concern and were aware that the Destination BrandScience process had been successfully conducted in other major destinations. They also understood that Palm Beach County did not have the media presence or overall awareness enjoyed by formidable and emerging competitors in Florida, the Caribbean and other national and international destinations.

The group wanted answers to questions such as: Do we understand how we are perceived as a leisure and business destination? Are we projecting the right message and image for this vast region to maximize our limited marketing funds?

The second point addresses a unique challenge for a destination the size of Palm Beach County. Larger than the states of Delaware and Rhode Island and reaching from its 47-mile Atlantic Ocean coastline to Lake Okeechobee and the Everglades, the destination is the largest county east of the Mississippi River. Some have even referred to Palm Beach County as an actual state, with 38 individual municipalities vying for a piece of the tourism pie.

That was the easy part and an important lesson for those considering the Destination BrandScience process; when it comes to an assessment of a community's image and possible changes in how the destination is projected to various audiences, whether leisure or business travelers, government officials or other local stakeholders, it is critically important to acknowledge the highly sensitive nature of the subject at hand.

The next few rounds of discussions and approvals required a greater effort. In a community with the history and cachet of Palm Beach, the common reaction would be: "if it ain't broke don't fix it," particularly when "the fix" might require an investment upward of six figures.

As the PBC CVB was preparing to issue the Request for Proposal (RFP), the first round of warning signs surfaced. Some in the community asked, "Are we really ready to embark on this, is it really necessary?" The seeming resistance to a project that might reveal some "inconvenient truths" was exacerbated by recent bad press concerning the PBC CVB and the Palm Beach County government which produced unanticipated flashing neon lights of caution.

Prior to Pesquera's arrival, a high-profile scandal at the PBC CVB and alleged cases of corruption involving county leadership had rocked the community to its very core. These events made national and international news and Pesquera did not realize that a complicated healing process was still taking place – one that involved nearly every major decision affecting the county's, and by default, the destination's image.

Therefore the process took much longer than anticipated. Pesquera realized that the county administration and the Tourism Development Council (TDC), an advisory board serving at the pleasure of the Palm Beach County Board of Commissioners, needed to have more confidence in a project entitled "Community Brand Assessment." For several months, the importance and value of the project continued to be reinforced through a series of one-on-one meetings with key influential members of these groups.

Potential challenges still persisted, some stemming from the well-earned pride by community leaders of this place called Palm Beach County. In their minds, this was and is universally known as one of the world's great luxury destinations. "You must have one of the easiest jobs in this county," said a well-heeled politician, "everyone knows Palm Beach around the country and around the world." Pesquera knew he needed to take bold action to remove any doubts that this was a vital step in the road to becoming "one of a kind." He needed a Tourism Summit!

The Tourism Summit. This had never been done in Palm Beach County, which was revolutionary, considering the area is considered the birthplace of Florida tourism. When the legendary industrial titan Henry M. Flagler came to Palm Beach in 1884, he referred to it as "a veritable paradise." Only a few years later, Flagler opened the Royal Poinciana Hotel, with over 1000 rooms, the Palm Beach property was recognized as the largest wooden structure in the world.

It would take more than a century before tourism officials finally determined it was time to move forward with an independent objective destination assessment. Structured as a full day discussion about Palm Beach County tourism, the Summit was open to the business community, media and local political leadership. It drew a standing-room-only crowd and included presentations by the PBC CVB and other TDC-funded entities (Sports Commission, Cultural Council and Film Commission).

More importantly, the program featured presentations by CEOs of competing destinations including the Miami CVB, the Hotel Association of the Island of St. Lucia in the Caribbean and the Center for Association Leadership. They spoke frankly about their own challenges and successes and how they viewed the destination of Palm Beach County. Presentations also included the Founder and Chairman of BrandStrategy, Inc. and the President of Zeigeist Consulting. Zeitgeist had recently completed the TDC's first-ever strategic plan which recommended Palm Beach County undergo a brand assessment. BrandStrategy Inc.'s presentation advanced the idea with a primer on the Destination

BrandScience process as adopted by the Destination Marketing Association International (DMAI).

The message was not what the audience thought they'd hear; that Palm Beach County was not the "top of mind" destination as some within the community had expected. The image was not as clear as one would like, and preoccupation with corruption and internal issues had taken focus away from the main mission of a DMO: the deployment of a comprehensive, research-based marketing strategy delivering compelling messages and imagery that resonate in the minds of customers.

Following the Tourism Summit, Pesquera strategically arranged one-on-one meetings with various members of the PBC CVB, TDC and the Palm Beach County Board of Commissioners, reinforcing the need to move forward with this project.

This extended process might be considered overkill in some destinations. But in communities with long and storied histories and a seemingly well established image, the DMO must be hypersensitive to the need for building alliances and garnering reliable support prior to launching the project.

The painstaking process of individual meetings, presentations at various board meetings and finally, hosting a major industry event aimed at challenging the status quo, is how Palm Beach County directed the preamble to the expert selection process and project launch. The Palm Beach County CVB Board of Directors provided exceptional leadership and support during the multi-year process.

It worked! Once the RFP was written and properly vetted, formal approvals by the various boards of the CVB, TDC and Board of County Commissioners occurred with relative ease.

The Brand Committee consisting of stakeholders, lodging industry executives and Palm Beach County officials, was wholly dedicated to the project's successful implementation. Also in partnership with Pesquera were Deputy County Administrator, Verdenia Baker, and the Executive Director of the TDC. Thanks to this successful community-wide collaboration, the Assessment and BrandPromise portions of the destination strategy were completed ahead of schedule.

Only a few months later, data mined for the project's independent research was quickly utilized for the PBC CVB's emergency Tourism Stimulus marketing campaign. Created to boost occupancies and Revenue per Available Room (RevPar) following the "small recession," the overwhelmingly positive results of the promotion resulted in Palm Beach County enjoying the fastest tourism recovery in Florida in 2010.

The growing number of high-profile publicity hits and full-color features in traditional and digital media outlets validate the thousands of daily visits to the newly created palmbeachfl.com website. Long reaching payoffs of the project are also evident in the 23 consecutive months of positive average daily rate growth (ADR) and 29 consecutive months of RevPar growth.

The Hospitality Sales and Marketing Association International (HSMAI) recognized the PBC CVB's efforts with its prestigious Gold Adrian Award, and named Pesquera one of the "Top 25 Most Extraordinary Minds in Sales and Marketing." ■

❑ The Destination BrandScience mindset needs to become an ongoing and integral part of the life of the destination for as long as it exists. The destination board and staff will have to make the brand a living and breathing part of its operation as it embarks on all of its activities.

❑ A destination should plan ahead to undertake this process and budget its money and time accordingly. Too many destinations try to squeeze this process in as just another part of "business as usual" during a hectic year. This process will take significant dedicated time, energy and senior staff manpower, even if an outside expert is used.

❑ Because of the political nature of destinations and the challenges in discussing touchy or politically explosive issues, it is recommended to retain an outside, impartial expert who can guide the process.

❑ A timetable and work plan should be established for a brand initiative with monthly updates and progress reports.

❑ Progress presentations should be made to the destination organization's board, community influencers and senior staff on a regular basis.

❑ A Destination Marketing Organization's CEO must be completely supportive of the Doctrine process and play an integral role in its development.

❑ A destination's board must be informed and totally supportive of the process, involved at appropriate times and eager to be a champion of the program when it is finished.

❑ A senior destination executive must be the partner responsible for the strategy and work closely with the outside expert as appropriate. This process should not be managed by a low level manager since that person may not have the credibility needed to make key decisions or to gain consensus at the appropriate times.

❏ To help facilitate buy in, it is recommended that the destination create a brand team that is comprised of a cross section of key leaders and board members with either strong marketing or brand management expertise. This will allow the opportunity to test ideas, concepts or proposed Promises to a sample of the community before going public.

❏ The brand's Promise should meet a variety of criteria and should enjoy widespread community acceptance when it is announced. Its purpose should not be to appease political interests or promote an agenda or it will not create the right guest experience, and community stakeholders will not embrace it.

❏ The Brand Guide should be completed, in writing, at the conclusion of the process. It should direct all the destination's activities and be reviewed and updated annually or every two years prior to the marketing plan and budget process. During the culturalization phase, the destination may need to commit additional resources on an annual basis to see that the Promise is being delivered and nurtured.

Chapter Three

Brand Assessment

*"An objective Assessment process looks
at a destination through the guest's eyes
to evaluate the community from
an objective perspective."*

The perception of a destination is all in the eyes of the guests. So, how does a Destination Marketing Organization (DMO) know where its destination stands today? The answers are revealed through a Brand Assessment. The Assessment is really like a Global Positioning System (GPS). A GPS tells you where you are and how to get where you want to go. Similarly, an Assessment tells the destination where it is in the minds of its target audiences and where the opportunities are to develop the optimal guest experiences and perceptions.

This disciplined evaluation examines a destination brand's current position, including an independent situation analysis of the marketplace, guests, competitors and relevant economic and industry conditions supported by demographic and psychographic data as well as relevant trends.

Be Real and Honest. DMOs are the paid professional boosters for their communities and may overlook their community's flaws and imperfections to focus on the city's perceived positive characteristics. The negative aspects of a community, homelessness, crime, downtown decay or even a weak number of guest attractions, may be ignored all together.

If a strategy for a Destination Brand is to be successful, there has to be candid dialogue about every aspect of a community's experience and product characteristics, both good and bad.

Before an Assessment begins, community representatives and stakeholders must acknowledge that their communities have definitive strengths and weaknesses. The participants, including elected leadership, must be willing to candidly discuss what makes the community unique and what aspects are impediments to its success as a destination.

Whatever positives are accentuated and highlighted, regardless of the value to the guest, the negatives must be considered equally.

The Need for an Objective Perspective. To evaluate the community from an objective perspective, the Assessment process sees a destination through the guest's eyes. The Brand Assessment process is designed to characterize the current perceptions of a Destination Brand based on factual and observable conclusions in a manner that precludes subjective prejudice. Just as an annual financial audit is required to verify the financial condition of an organization, an Assessment of the brand is required to verify a destination's actual image and perception in the guests' minds.

Stakeholders and guests are often at odds over the brand perception of a destination. The Brand Assessment will help bring these differing viewpoints to a consensus.

This is an important reason to contract with an outside destination brand expert, advisor or community leader who can be totally objective about the destination. It will also be necessary to contract with a qualified research firm to conduct the third party research relative to guests and influencers such as meeting professionals. The methodology employed by these firms ensure that the results are impartial and honest.

According to Greg Dunn, professor of hospitality marketing and travel industry research expert, "it is now more important than ever that destinations understand how they are perceived in the marketplace. Solid research drives solid strategy and Destination BrandScience is the right approach. It brings together market research (guests, influencers and stakeholders) and includes the development of an effective Promise. Working with Visit Estes Park, we combined guests' perceptions, market trends and community perspectives with BrandStrategy, Inc.'s scientific approach to develop a new destination strategy."

How to Apply the Brand Assessment Methodology. The Assessment process evaluates a brand's perceived position and builds consensus consistent with guests' reality. The most important goal of the Assessment is to determine how guests, influencers and stakeholders feel about a destination. The methodology has been designed to assess:

▲ Key aspects of the destination's brand image

▲ Current business

▲ Industry trends, present and future

▲ Relevant critical success factors, strengths and weaknesses that may impact the Destination Brand's performance

The Assessment's objective is to take the guest's perspective and identify critical brand issues. DMOs may be dismayed to learn that stakeholders and guests are often at odds with the stakeholders' perception of their destination. While a mayor and city leadership may see the community as "on the move with dynamic new development," a guest may see a city as "outdated and unexciting." These issues are to be expected in varying degrees.

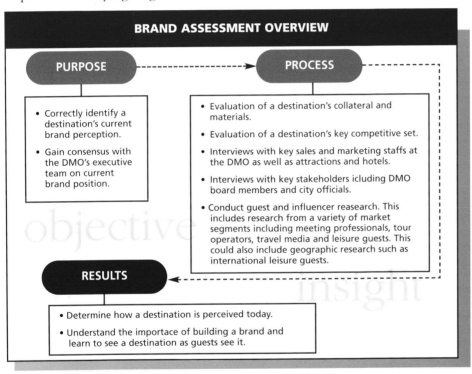

BRAND ASSESSMENT OVERVIEW

PURPOSE

- Correctly identify a destination's current brand perception.
- Gain consensus with the DMO's executive team on current brand position.

PROCESS

- Evaluation of a destination's collateral and materials.
- Evaluation of a destination's key competitive set.
- Interviews with key sales and marketing staffs at the DMO as well as attractions and hotels.
- Interviews with key stakeholders icluding DMO board members and city officials.
- Conduct guest and influencer reasearch. This includes research from a variety of market segments including meeting professionals, tour operators, travel media and leisure guests. This could also include geographic research such as international leisure guests.

RESULTS

- Determine how a destination is perceived today.
- Understand the importace of building a brand and learn to see a destination as guests see it.

Key Assessment Issues. The following outlines selected issues that should be addressed in the Assessment:

▲ What is the first word to come to mind when guests and the public think of the destination brand?

▲ What is the consensus of opinion regarding the destination's image and future perception?

▲ What are the destination's strengths and weaknesses (internal and external perceptions)?

▲ What are the destination's strongest positive benefits or attributes for guests and influencers?

▲ How is the Destination's Brand currently positioned?

▲ Who are the destination's current and future guests and what other travel segments should be targeted for future marketing and promotions?

▲ How do guests and meeting professionals do business with the destination brand?

▲ What market segments have the highest potential for generating visitations, meeting planner support and tour operator interest?

▲ What brand identities are reflected by the destination's guest services and convention services, etc.?

▲ What are the guest's perceptions of the destination based on an audit of the social media?

▲ What is the destination's visual "sense of arrival" wherever guests arrive, i.e., highway, airport, etc.?

▲ What messages do external media, local and national, traditional and digital, convey?

▲ What messages does the DMO's public relations activity convey?

▲ Does the destination currently have a Promise commitment? Is there a perceived Promise?

▲ What Promise is currently being communicated by the DMO to current and potential guests, influencers and stakeholders?

▲ Do different parts of the community (such as the chamber of commerce, city and the DMO) communicate an identical Promise and message to their respective audiences? Do they have their own proprietary messages?

▲ What other brands could the destination associate with to improve its brand equity?

A DMO is often the chief marketing authority for the community and image-maker for the destination. As such, its messages are powerful influencers. This is why the Assessment begins with a comprehensive review of the DMO's marketing materials, including:

▲ Brochures and other promotional messages

▲ Media kits and releases

▲ Images in all formats and media

▲ Sales kits and guides for meeting planners, tour operators and travel agents

▲ Business cards and stationery

▲ Trade show displays including booth themes

▲ Direct mail and email promotional distributions, newsletters, sales flashes, etc.

▲ The DMO's website and social media presence

▲ DMO membership sales materials

▲ DMO board materials

What is the Visual Message? In reviewing these materials, DMO representatives should ask the following questions:

▲ What are the destination's primary visual themes? (Examples: fun, escapism, adventure, romance, etc.)

▲ Is there message consistency across all media and how are messages conveyed?

▲ Are there discrepancies in the messaging between different market segments?

▲ Are deliberate messages avoided?

▲ Is a Promise being conveyed directly or indirectly in the destination's promotional messages and printed materials?

▲ How are other agencies in the community – city government, chamber of commerce, hotels and attractions – reacting to these messages? Are they consistent with what those organizations are emphasizing?

▲ How did the DMO develop these messages, and how long has the current campaign been public? Has it changed?

▲ Is there an inconsistency with what the DMO knows the destination to be and the actual destination product? How much of it is "fluff" compared to reality?

After the information has been collected and scrutinized, a concise summary should be prepared with the key findings comparing the current with past and future plans and performances.

Three Areas of Research. The key functional elements of an Assessment are:

Marketing strategy evaluation
Evaluate a destination's marketing plan and its effectiveness.

Community research
Interviews and surveys with key local stakeholders.

Market research
Surveys with guests, meeting professionals, tour operators, digital intermediaries and media representatives.

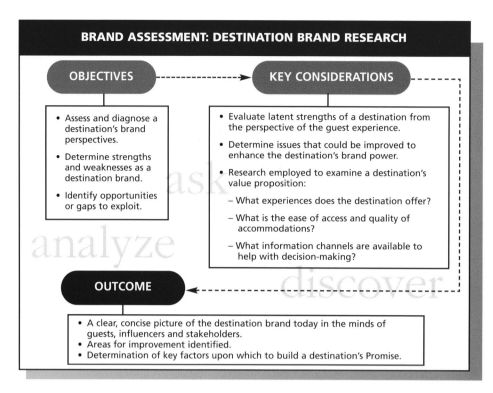

It is extremely important not to just get information related to the destination itself, but also research that compares a destination with three to five key competitors and their "best demonstrated practices."

Marketing Strategy Evaluation. The purpose of examining the DMO's current marketing plan is to gain insight into the consistency, commitment and effectiveness of the current and proposed marketing programs. These questions help uncover valuable answers:

▲ What channels of distribution and communication are being utilized? How are we getting our message to our target audiences?

▲ Who are we targeting and why?

▲ What is the reach and frequency of these programs?

▲ What is the destination's social media strategy?

▲ Do we measure the effectiveness of any programs? If so, what information is available? If not, why not?

▲ Who competes for the destination's guests? Who is our primary, secondary and tertiary competition?

▲ Which destinations are likely to be future competitors?

▲ What is the concise positioning statement that summarizes the marketing goals?

▲ What are the major expenditures and measured results for each of the past three years?

After the information has been collected and scrutinized, a concise summary should be prepared with the key findings comparing the current with past and future plans and performances.

Community Research: Gain Insight from Local Stakeholders.

Stakeholder destination brand research serves as a diagnostic tool to identify exactly where the destination is now, and what can be done to enhance its position in the future. Data gained from stakeholder research findings is crucial to the success of a destination brand initiative.

Interviews with local stakeholders are one of the most valuable and informative aspects of an Assessment process. In addition to gaining stakeholder insights, the DMO can also generate support for the Doctrine process. This buy-in will become a valuable asset when implementing the Promise.

A DMO should compile a list of all stakeholders to be interviewed by staff and the expert involved with the project, including:

▲ Public officials

▲ Government officials, including selected city and county managers and members of the economic development agency

▲ Chamber of commerce executives

▲ Hospitality leaders, including hotel general managers, directors of marketing and sales, attractions, restaurants, transportation companies and cultural institutions

▲ State tourism officials and boards

In all communities, there are supporters and detractors of the tourism industry. It is critical that these detractors be included in the process and have a chance to discuss their views of the destination.

While this might be viewed as pandering to the detractors, it actually is an extremely valuable exercise that often gleans insight into a destination brand and the DMO's involvement with it. Additionally, when the Doctrine is completed, detractors are much more likely to support the overall effort knowing that their views were seriously considered in the development of the program.

Once completed, it is important to list the types and numbers of the interviewees in the Assessment report's appendix. Readers should understand the breadth of the community's involvement and the variety of individuals who contributed to the overall strategy.

Community Insights and Confidentiality. Although stakeholder interviews may be the most time-consuming aspect in the completion of the Assessment, they should not be rushed. The overall process is likely to take at least one to two months depending upon the size of the community and the complexity of the destination.

Elected leaders, particularly city council members, may be reluctant to express views that may alienate fellow officials, and therefore should have their insights nurtured on an individual basis. For example, a downtown area may be a perceived weakness in the destination, but a councilperson may not want to express that viewpoint in a public meeting.

It is important to understand that most elected leaders appreciate the opportunity to be candid and honest about their community, as long as they feel secure in knowing their confidentiality is protected. Hospitality industry leaders also appreciate the chance to open up and discuss obstacles to the destination sales effort and are usually pleased that the DMO is being straightforward in discussing these issues.

While a DMO needs candor in gathering this information, it should also respect the confidential nature of these discussions. If a brand expert is guiding the process, some interviews may be conducted without the DMO's presence in order to protect the confidentiality of stakeholders. It is especially important to protect the identity of any individual stakeholder related to any quotes which become part of the Assessment Report.

Throughout the Assessment process, it is best to conduct stakeholder interviews using a set of uniform questions. However, if the interviewee goes down a path that is informative and insightful, it's best to allow them to communicate his/her thoughts.

> The objective of this Assessment is to gain as much "truth" from key stakeholders regarding the destination, so the DMO can move beyond the protective nature of community leaders and learn what is really on their minds.

When the interviews are completed, the interviewer should prepare a matrix of responses to determine any recurring "themes" in the responses. Is there a repetition of specific strengths and weaknesses? Are common terms used to describe the destination? Is there a discrepancy between what community leaders want the destination to be and what it actually is?

Market Research: Gain Insight from a destination's various customers (guests, meeting professionals, tour operators and travel media). Ultimately, the most critical aspect of the Brand Assessment process is the guest, consumer and influencer feedback. Often, intermediaries, including tour operators or travel media, come between a DMO and the guest. While intermediaries should be interviewed, the most interesting and fun part of the Assessment comes from working with the guests themselves. When we refer to guests, we mean those from out of town as well as local residents and their house guests.

Ultimately, it is the guests who pay the bills for a destination's tourism industry. However, many DMOs have little to no dialogue with guests on a regular basis.

For a truly impartial Assessment, it is wise to have a qualified research company conduct the guest market research component of the process. For example, if a DMO's key feeder market is Dallas/Fort Worth, it is recommended that internet surveys or focus groups from that area be conducted.

Perceptual Mapping. A tool that MarketVision Research uses to measure and represent guest perceptions is called perceptual mapping. By researching consumers' associations of key attributes with various destinations, a perceptual map can be created, like the example below. This map is sometimes called a point and vector solution, and can contain a wealth of information. It illustrates the following:

▲ The relationship among destination features or attributes

▲ How much each destination is associated with certain attributes

▲ How similar competing destinations are perceived by a target audience

In essence, it illustrates what a destination is associated with, what a destination potentially could be associated with, and what would be difficult to be associated with. For example, the following perceptual map tells us that Destination A is most associated with a relaxing and romantic atmosphere, whereas Destinations C and D are both associated with pampering, an upscale atmosphere and safety. Therefore, Destination D would need to carefully consider how best to position itself on these attributes, as Destination C is already seen as closely associated with these attributes. The map also shows a disconnect for Destination B, which is perceived to be naturally beautiful but, because of this perception, is also perceived to offer less to do from an attraction and amenities standpoint.

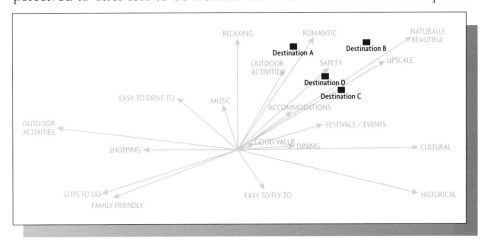

These maps and the brand intelligence gathered through the Assessment provide the informational foundation to inform a destination's

brand initiative. Once the Assessment is completed, destinations have the intelligence necessary to identify initial conclusions, namely:

▲ Your brand perceptions compared to your competitor's brand perceptions

▲ Key drivers of brand choice

▲ Points of brand differentiation with which a destination is best associated

A later step of the destination Assessment process comes after the strategy for the brand initiative is launched. This approach monitors and evaluates the brand execution to ensure that it is reaching its intended audience and is resonating. Without evaluating the program, there is no way of knowing the return on the investment.

According to Don Morgan, of GMA Research, guests are often contacted and asked a series of diagnostic questions to determine what's working and what's not with respect to a brand initiative. Additionally, a destination can conduct research based on its finalized Promise. Future research can be completed on an ongoing basis to determine its guests' perception of how the destination is delivering on its Promise.

Though there are multiple methods for collecting the intelligence needed in the Assessment work, the Internet lends itself extremely well to the destination brand research process. The reasons the Internet works well for the brand research process are based on the following:

▲ It is the most time, cost and reporting-efficient way to interview guests, consumers, meeting professionals, etc., across target markets.

▲ It allows for the graphic representation of destination images, messages, slogans and marketing materials.

▲ This method lends itself extremely well to re-contacting respondents to test branding positions and monitor and evaluate the program.

Destination Brand Research Essentials. Research is imperative to the overall success of a destination brand initiative. Without it, you do not know what share of guests' minds you own, could own or potentially never could own. Through destination brand research, you can uncover how to increase mind share in order to grow and maintain visitation. You will also have accountability measures to address stakeholders' questions and concerns.

1. **Determine how all types of guests perceive and feel about the destination.** Asking guests questions such as how they perceive the destination in terms of getting better, staying the same or becoming worse, or do they feel the destination is equal to or better than other destinations, can uncover predictable attitudes and perceptions.

2. **A brand is a Promise to gather perceptions from all guest segments.** In the Promise phase, once a Promise is drafted, it can be regularly tested with guests and prospective guests (as well as stakeholder segments) in focus groups, in on-site interviews or via an online research methodology. Feedback on reactions to the Promise is critical prior to finalization, acceptance and implementation/culturalization.

3. **Design survey questions to engage guests' feelings.** As noted earlier, questions designed to elicit and measure/gauge guest feelings and attitudes are just as or more important than behavioral questions designed to measure frequency of visit, expenditure patterns, etc. Knowing and understanding how guests "feel" is of paramount importance.

4. **Monitor brand effectiveness.** Measure and benchmark satisfaction and loyalty levels. Research identifies critical elements of the destination experience as well as competitors' relative performance. Routine, periodic research is required to gauge the destination brand's ability to deliver on its Promise over time and track changes toward any of its inherent brand attributes.

5. **Evaluate website and social media effectiveness.** This evaluation is designed to provide an objective measurement to gauge the "brand" effectiveness of a website by taking into consideration some important applications of basic brand-building principles. The evaluation will also examine a brand's website from the perspective of its intended target audience. The criteria used in the evaluation process are designed to assess guests' experiences and the potential to meet brand expectations.

Professional focus group facilities allow DMO executives and board members to watch the interviews of the pre-screened guests behind a one-way mirror. Videos can be used to present findings and conclusions to those who were not able to personally attend the interviews. These sessions can be invaluable for discovering honest, true perceptions of the destination's brand.

If cost is an issue, a DMO may consider sharing costs with another similarly inclined agency also undertaking an Assessment. For example, two DMOs wanted to conduct focus groups in London, an important international market for both destinations. Due to the costs, the individual DMOs could not do it on their own. By agreeing to select participants based on similar demographics, the agencies were able to conduct successful London-based focus groups and received the much-needed data within their allotted budgets.

Influencer Insights. In addition to guests, influencers (including meeting professionals, tour operators and travel media) are critical to the Assessment process. They are often the primary "sellers" of the destination to their customers or readers, and have strong impressions about the destination brand.

These groups should be interviewed separately, as they may have issues unrelated to other companies. Again, similar themes may be identified, and these thoughts should be incorporated into a matrix while not divulging the individual identity of the respondents.

Enlightening Wisdom. At the conclusion of the Assessment process, which may vary in length and complexity, a DMO will often find moments of enlightenment. The dichotomy of perception and reality will come to light and a DMO may, for the first time, discover how guests and stakeholders really feel about their destination. Sometimes, this will confirm what a DMO already knows to be true, or provides concrete "evidence" to substantiate concerns that have been voiced for some time.

The most important goal of the Assessment is to understand how all of a destination's customers (guests, influencers and stakeholders) feel about a destination's brand. The Assessment should be a mirror that gives insight into the soul of the destination and prepares the way for the DMO to begin development of the next step: the essence of the Destination Brand Doctrine – The BrandPromise Commitment. ∎

Brand Insight

Estes Park

In the case of Estes Park, the destination's most effective tool was the partnership between Visit Estes Park (the DMO), the Brand Team and the rest of the Estes Park community. Their Brand Team was comprised of committed individuals from the DMO, the Town Board of Trustees, Rocky Mountain National Park as well as representatives from a variety of businesses and local associations.

From the beginning of the project, the Brand Team was heavily involved in every phase and spent hours offering their interpretations, thoughts and ideas. The Brand Assessment was essential groundwork for gaining community buy-in. The Estes Park team identified a variety of opportunities for uniqueness, and each opportunity was triangulated by at least two to three robust pieces of research. From those opportunities, Estes Park Promise concepts were built.

For example, the Brand Team learned that their destination generally had one "season" and did not have a current (community-wide) strategy to create a year-round destination. Through their year-round guest study, however, Estes Park knew that guest satisfaction markedly declined in their "on-season" and that, in fact, guests had extremely high satisfaction levels during the "off-season." The necessary paradigm shift was to move away from this on versus off-season mentality, and toward an idea that the destination is always in season, always ready for guests. The recognition of this internal seasonal mindset was strongly supported by the Brand Team, shared with a variety of community members and key influencers, and consequently eagerly accepted by those groups.

Other Promise concepts were approached in a similar manner. Their Brand Team identified various opportunities in the destination, which was always supported by the research, and created a concept that became an inspirational element of the Promise. The Promise was formed directly from these fenceposts, and then widely shared with the community.

Hundreds of community members were given an opportunity to learn about the Brand Team's discoveries and ideas. Early on, this method created a culture of support for the Estes Park's brand strategy. According to Kirby Nelson, Stakeholder Relations & Communications Manager of Visit Estes Park, Colorado, "Our Brand Team was a significant reason behind our success: how hard they worked, the diversity in their experiences and their commitment to distinguishing Estes Park as a unique and distinctive destination. Equally as important was our level of community engagement."

From the beginning of the process, key community influencers and groups were involved in learning about the Brand Team's work. Their input, feedback and ultimately, their support helped integrate the destination brand strategy across a wide spectrum. From tourism and business associations, to town government and staff, to lodging and restaurant management teams, to the educational constituents and other community organizations, their Promise was introduced to – and accepted by – the destination. As Kirby Nelson explained, "Due to the hard work and commitment to teamwork from our Brand Team, we never once had anyone say that our strategy was off track." ■

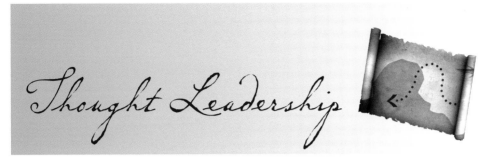

❏ An objective, independent assessment is required for a destination to select its future strategic direction.

❏ Retain a research firm or designate an internal research executive to oversee and implement the destination research process.

❏ Prepare an executive summary of all previous research completed over the last three years before any new research begins. It is essential to understand what research has been completed, so that any new research will be helpful in completing a comprehensive Brand Assessment. This includes a review of all brand communications, marketing plans and existing market and guest research.

❏ Evaluate key aspects of the destination's brand image, current and forecast business and industry factors. Identify pertinent success drivers, including strengths and weaknesses that could impact the brand's future performance.

❏ Identify "best demonstrated practices" of other destinations and commercial brands that could provide insights for the destination brand initiative.

❏ Design a questionnaire for guest and non-guest research and identify the appropriate interview formats: on-site intercepts, online focus group or telephone surveys.

❏ Prepare a written summary of findings and conclusions. Present these findings to the BrandTeam and gain consensus on the results reflecting the current destination brand position.

❏ Complete the Brand Assessment report and proceed to the next stage – development of the BrandPromise Commitment.

Notes

Chapter Four

BrandPromise

"The Promise drives destination brand success and long term competitive advantage."

You've passed the first milestone on your journey towards the development of a Genuine Brand. At this stage, it is vital to grasp the meaning of how to *think like a brand*. Thinking like a brand requires a different perspective than how one thinks about day-to-day business. This point of view is grounded in a destination brand's Promise.

The Promise is the **internal** rallying cry of a Genuine Brand and expresses the spirit of its distinctiveness. It is a destination brand's value proposition – its commitment to its guests – defined as the essence of the benefits, both functional and emotional, that current and potential guests can expect to receive throughout the destination experience.

A Promise is absolutely fundamental to the creation, development or enhancement of a new or existing brand. If a destination brand aspires to become a Genuine Brand in the minds of its guests, influencers and stakeholders, the right Promise is essential. A Promise communicates three essential attributes:

1. **Something will be done**

2. **An expressed assurance**

3. **A perception of future excellence**

The Promise is the Foundation of a Brand's Experience.

The right Promise is required to become a Genuine Brand and deliver a distinctive experience. There are three principles to achieving the right Promise for everyone involved in a brand (guests, stakeholders and influencers).

▲ Provide a unique **experience** with products and services that enhance guests' lives.

▲ Achieve community **partnership**, passion and support for a Promise.

▲ Create a perception of **exceptional value** and distinctive benefits.

As you can see, creating the right Promise is not just about an advertising message or a new logo. It's much more than any of these. When asked if an organization has a Promise, executives frequently say: "Yes, we have a branding program," or "We've gone through a whole branding exercise."

Branding is usually about messages and images and not the ALL ENCOMPASSING experience.

What we are talking about is creating a Promise, not about branding. This is not to say that branding for some organizations has not included a Promise.

Most of the time branding means a new message, image or promotional campaign and not a comprehensive commitment to the entire experience that a destination provides guests, stakeholders and influencers internally and externally.

Any and every successful branding or brand initiative, campaign or program must answer the question: Is this about "substance;" that is, is this about a Promise, or is it "hype?" If the answer is substance, then you're ready to enhance people's lives.

Enhancing Guests' Lives.
The first question we think about with potential destination clients is whether they are sincerely interested in enhancing their guests' lives.

How is your destination brand enhancing its guests' lives today? Here are some questions to ask:

▲ Do your representatives use your products and services as much as your best customers do?

▲ Do your guests talk positively about your brand to their friends as if they own it?

▲ Do you hire representatives who have the emotional ability to make your influencers, stakeholders and guests feel special?

▲ Does every representative really care about how his or her guests feel?

▲ Do your guests create their own positive descriptors for your brand such as the "Costco run" for Costco or "Tar-shay" for Target? Do they tattoo your brand on their bodies like Harley-Davidson customers?

▲ Does your destination treat guests better than they expected?

▲ Do you provide a no-hassle, nonconfrontational, unconditional guarantee of satisfaction?

▲ Would you force your mother to navigate an automated phone system when she calls your destination organization?

▲ Do you have a Promise that every representative knows?

What an Internal Promise Is and Is Not. A strong Promise serves as the guiding star for a destination and directs its marketing program on the transformational path to Genuine Brand distinction. To stand the test of time, a destination brand needs to stand for something larger than just a utilitarian benefit. Destinations have to realize that they must examine their image if they desire to occupy a distinctive and valued position in the minds of their guests, influencers and stakeholders.

A Promise is not a description of product attributes, such as a destination having theme parks or national monuments. The Promise is usually a short paragraph comprised of three sentences or less.

The Promise answers three fundamental questions:

▲ What should our destination's experience be all about?

▲ What distinguishes our products and services from competitors'?

▲ What is superior about the value we offer our guests?

Tourism Vancouver's Promise is as relevant today as when it was first launched in 2005, particularly since guests' expectations have evolved due to Vancouver's growing popularity and reputation since the Olympics. Their Promise states, "The Vancouver experience will exceed guests' expectations. We will deliver superior value within a spectacular destination that is safe, exciting and welcoming to everyone."

In order to support these tenets, Tourism Vancouver has prioritized a number of initiatives and programs as outlined in the Brand Insight at the end of this chapter.

For a destination brand to stand apart from competitors, especially in the minds and wallets of guests, the Promise must communicate its meaning clearly. At its core, it must communicate a lock-tight commitment that the anticipated experience will occur with a distinguishable perception of future excellence.

▲ A Promise is not a mission statement.

▲ A mission statement describes what an organization does; a Promise states how an organization wants its customers or guests to feel. A Promise connects deeply with the consumer and defines the destination, not in terms of function or purpose, but its ability to offer a meaningful experience that is unique and one that enhances the quality of guests' lives in some way.

▲ A Promise is also sometimes confused with a vision statement.

▲ A vision statement, which has a useful role with a destination, is focused on the future of the organization.

A Promise commitment accomplishes something more profound than either a mission or vision statement. It provides a clear and meaningful internal definition for the destination in an emotionally connected way that defines its intended distinctiveness. The intent of the Promise is an expressed assurance that something will occur with a clear perception of excellence.

The Promise Reflects the Destination's Character and Distinctive Experience. A successful destination Promise combines descriptive and meaningful words that truly reflect the destination's essential character and provides a distinctive experience that holds real value and appeal.

The key descriptive words that a destination can use to assemble its Promise are often the same words that were discovered during the Assessment process. Guests generally have an accurate picture of a destination's current experience and the corresponding adjectives to describe how it makes them feel. The words in the Promise should be carefully selected based on their emotional power, as well as the ability to connect the guest with the destination in a distinctive and truthful way.

The true value of the Assessment process is not just to validate what a destination may already know, but also to learn what it doesn't know about the destination experience. A Promise should never be a forced and uncomfortable description of a community's essence. In fact, when a successful Promise is crafted, community stakeholders should be able to fully understand and grasp the words and feel that the essential character of a destination is conveyed. But more importantly, should the Promise be read to a guest, it should elicit the same feelings.

It's about MAKING and KEEPING a Promise with people. It goes beyond writing it down – it's about LIVING THE PROMISE!

An effective Promise should also have an aspirational quality to it. While the Promise should reflect the destination as it stands now, it should have an element that encourages the destination to reach beyond itself while being true to its roots. But it should be noted, that, aspiration is not the same as fantasy. A struggling downtown, even during its best days, will never have the same energy as New York City. Even terrific theme parks may not compare to a Disney World experience. While being aspirational is a good quality, being distinctive and honest in the Promise is also critically important.

A brand's Promise is not an advertising message.

In fact, although a Promise should be well known and embraced by all representatives of a destination, as well as the board leadership, the intent is not to be featured in advertising or even collateral.

The Promise should drive appropriate advertising and promotional messages and brochure creation, but the Promise in its literal form should not be promoted as a slogan. It is best used as an internal guiding star in which all other creative messages are developed.

FedEx's advertised message is: "absolutely, positively, overnight." However, their Promise relates to the benefit its customers expect: Immediate gratification.

Every traveler's best friend is a bottle of water. Imagine a bottled water that is a Genuine Brand. Essentia's super hydrating water® is one of them.

Essentia is more than just enhanced water. It's water that completely and thoroughly does what water is *supposed* to do – hydrates you and helps you stay healthy.

The brand differentiates itself by the proprietary Essentia Process, which is a method that results in water that is more mineral rich with optimum alkalinity and higher pH. It gives you more of what you need to thrive and helps bring your body back into balance – helping to support normal blood pressure, restful sleep, heart health, muscle strength and more.

This makes Essentia the brand of choice for those seeking water's restorative power, amplified. Essentia's sleek logo and bottle label prominently feature this restorative power by highlighting the ideal pH of 9.5 and emphasizing the plus (+), which draws a stronger connection to the added benefits.

Essentia's customers aren't the only ones who rave about the water. With leadership from CEO Ken Uptain, every Essentia employee is fully invested in the brand's success. Each is an ambassador for the brand and takes personal responsibility for making sure their Brand Promise comes alive at all times. Their Promise states, "Dedicated to enhancing our customers' health and vitality. Bottled with integrity, assuring consistency and quality in every bottle of Essentia Water. Trusted since 1998 to deliver the best hydration and taste."

Everyone delivers this Promise the "Essentia Way," making sure that the brand is in alignment with its Promise of integrity, consistency and quality. They are its biggest supporters – and the Promise has paid off, with over 20,000 bottles of Essentia consumed daily. In fact, it is the number one selling bottled water brand in the natural channel nationwide. Today, you can find Essentia in most major grocery stores, from Whole Foods to Publix and online through Amazon.com.

So there you have it – distinctiveness is always a key to success. An authentic enhancement to water combined with a successful strategy results in a Genuine Brand that consistently delivers on its Promise.

As Orin Smith, retired CEO of Starbucks said in *The BrandPromise,* "There is an enormous difference between talking about a Promise and making and keeping a Promise to customers, associates and shareholders. The Promise philosophy focuses on the difference between slogans or taglines and putting your heart and soul into your Promise."

The PromiseRule®. Everyone's heard of the Golden Rule: Do unto others as you would have others do unto you. While the Golden Rule is important, we believe that it's time to raise the bar. The new standard for Genuine Brands is the PromiseRule: Treat others *better* than they expect to be treated. Success and competitive advantage are all about exceeding guests' expectations.

> Treat others BETTER than they EXPECT to be TREATED!

Compare Beliefs to Perceptions. The following chart illustrates the Promise methodology. It requires a bit of self-examination, exploration and objective thinking. This insight is then mixed with the relevant and meaningful qualities found in an organization's vision, mission and values, as well as the guest and stakeholder knowledge acquired from the Assessment. It is also necessary to examine the current culture of the DMO in order to gain an understanding of its existing beliefs. An organization's beliefs can be discovered by how it communicates, acts and decides what direction to take.

In scrutinizing communications – internal and external-printed, audio and video – look for any of the following brand clues:

▲ Strategic direction

▲ Key messages or themes

▲ Consistency of image and messages

▲ Tone or personality

This information should be compared to the data and findings gleaned from the Assessment for similarities and differences. The key to this analysis is the comparison of the destination organization's beliefs to its messages and the resulting guest perception of the destination and its brand.

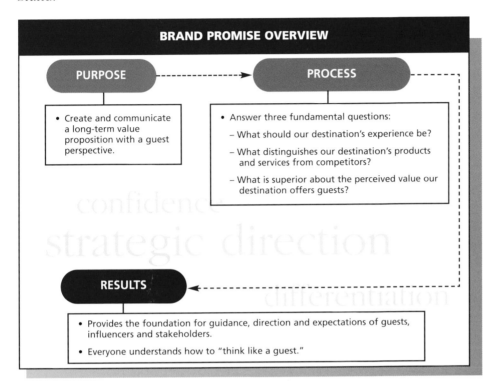

How the Brand Team Works Towards the Promise. The most efficient way for a destination to develop its Promise is for a Brand Team, which is usually comprised of key destination executives and knowledgeable community leaders, to come together and first review the Assessment findings. After posting the key Assessment conclusions for the destination on flip charts, each Brand Team member should craft a three-sentence proposed Promise. Each Promise should be copied onto the flip chart and left in a visible place for participants to look at and consider.

The group should then form a consensus on the key elements of their Promise concept even though the exact wording may not be clear. This may be the time to interview advertising or public relations executives for their input. These key elements then can be fashioned by a single person and later emailed to participants for consideration. It is important that this process, while critical, should not be drawn out or turned into a lengthy discussion. Often the first thoughts and insights are the most useful in the process. A drawn out discussion often "over thinks" the issues and muddles the outcome. The entire process should also be done outside the glare of the public spotlight until there is consensus. If the Promise turns into something that is fashionable and politically correct instead of its desired outcome, then the process has been wasted.

Ultimately, the Promise should reflect a balance between the aspirations of the brand, as well as the reality of what the brand is capable of delivering to its guests. It's important to note that a Promise should be aspirational enough to reach for the stars with the understanding that a successful destination's Promise reflects a constant migration journey to fulfill their commitments.

After a destination's Brand Team has agreed on the Promise and its wording, it is wise to "test market" it with key stakeholders in a quiet manner. These should include elected city leadership and the destination's senior staff and board of directors. It should also include influential members of the hospitality community. If detractors of the destination and the hospitality community were a part of the Brand Assessment process, it is suggested that they too be briefed on the Promise before it becomes public. The more "buy-in" on the wording and nature of Promise will ensure its acceptance and buy-in by the community at large. The last thing a destination wants or needs is to have stakeholders publicly denounce the Promise before it has a chance to take flight.

As the chart below illustrates, when an organization can rise above the daily business operations and capture a place in guests' and consumers' minds, a gestalt if you will, then it has a chance to be something really special – a distinctive brand! The Walt Disney brand is not about theme parks or movies. It is about creating magical, happy feelings. Coca-Cola is not a soft drink, but is instead a cool refreshment. Coke's current theme line "Open Happiness" is a great example of how a Genuine Brand messages its Promise.

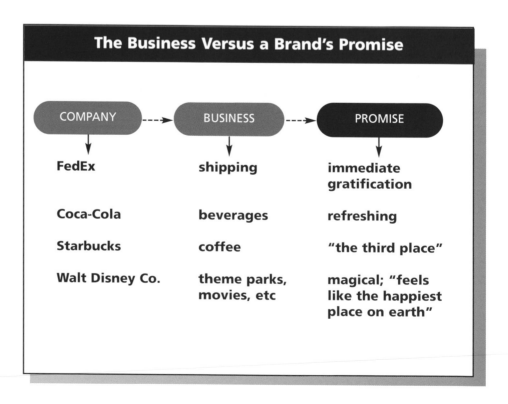

The Business Versus a Brand's Promise

COMPANY	BUSINESS	PROMISE
FedEx	shipping	immediate gratification
Coca-Cola	beverages	refreshing
Starbucks	coffee	"the third place"
Walt Disney Co.	theme parks, movies, etc	magical; "feels like the happiest place on earth"

A vitally important aspect of the BrandPromise Commitment to consider is that it is not just about defining the physical aspects of the destination, but creating an expectation of experience once the guest arrives.

When creating the Promise, it is important to ask, "What does the guest think is different about our destination when compared to our competitors?" The answer makes it possible for a destination to consider what it might do to further the perception of distinctiveness in the guest's minds, keeping in mind that the brand's perceived differentiation is a lifelong quest, not just the "idea of a the month."

A destination continues to evolve with new developments and infrastructure, much of it beyond the decision-making powers of a destination. As a destination creates itself anew as the years pass, so will the destination brand. If a city council embraces the concept of a destination Promise, they will hopefully make good decisions that will enhance and further the Promise and its intended experience. On the other hand, if development goes against what the established Promise commitment is, it can damage the destination and violate the destination's Promise with the guest. For example: If a quiet resort community becomes a congested metropolis, it disturbs the destination's brand integrity. That is why during the Assessment process, elected officials should have complete and total understanding of why a destination's Promise is not a marketing tactic, but a universal guidepost for the community.

There is nothing more valuable to guests than memories of feeling great. Create memorable experiences.

When You Experience a Destination's Promise. The destination's Promise comes to life when it is understood by each and everyone associated with the destination (its staff, members, employees and stakeholders). The brand comes alive when the Promise is delivered with flawless execution and the highest level of performance.

When the guest benefits from the delivery of a destination's Promise, the brand is real.

Genuine Brands make a Promise and they deliver that Promise consistently, enthusiastically and at the guest's convenience. A Genuine Brand creates relationships with guests centered on its Promise. The power of a Promise is based on what guests say about a destination brand to their friends and about their feelings toward the brand. Word of mouth can be one of the most important determinants of a brand's ultimate success. ■

Brand Insight

Delivering on a Destination Promise
Vancouver, British Columbia

Genuine Brands, like Tourism Vancouver, change the paradigm in their market sector. In other words, they change the model in their business so that they become perceived as a distinctive and one-of-a-kind destination – not just one of many. The following insight provides a revealing perspective related to this brand success.

Making a Promise is an exciting prospect. For Vancouver, Canada, the process of creating and fulfilling its Promise has had such an impact, it most likely changed the course of the city's history.

The lovely coastal city has been recognized as one of the best places in the world to live and continues to grow as a popular tourist attraction. Vancouver also boasts that it is one of the most ethnically and linguistically diverse cities in Canada with 52% of the population speaking a first language other than English.

In preparation for the 2010 Olympic and Paralympic Winter Games, Tourism Vancouver developed its Promise as part of the Destination BrandScience process. Because the Promise is defined as "the essence of the benefits, both functional and emotional, that current and potential guests can expect to receive," tourism officials realized this type of commitment required a great deal of advance work.

The good news is that Vancouver's gold medal performance as Olympic host to the world exceeded everyone's expectations. It is the city's continued dedication to the fulfillment of its Promise that is making the kind of new history any city would envy.

Delivering the Promise. When you think of a brand, you often think of consumer goods. Yet destinations need to subscribe to the same principles of BrandScience. In fact, the challenge becomes even greater when you're creating a destination experience.

Though visual identity is the face of a brand, its Promise is its heart. When Tourism Vancouver launched its new Promise and identity in 2005, the goal was simple yet ambitious: to deliver on a commitment of how the organization wants guests to feel when they visit Vancouver. Following the principles of Destination BrandScience, their strategy was designed as a compass that would guide the destination marketing organization (DMO), and the broader Vancouver tourism community, in ensuring that it aligned business activities with a real Promise focused on integrity and depth.

In anticipation of an unprecedented decade of opportunity leading up to hosting the 2010 Olympic and Paralympic Winter Games, the expansion of the Vancouver Convention and Exhibition Centre and emerging tourism markets, Vancouver knew it was time to recreate and revamp the brand. The results speak for themselves.

Some 3.5 billion people witnessed part of the Vancouver games either through television or the Internet, introducing the city, province and country to hundreds of untapped markets. Prior to the games, people had heard of Vancouver, but did not necessarily know about Vancouver. The Olympics and the accompanying mass of media exposure changed that. In fact, even today in the aftermath of the games, the city is experiencing tremendous media attention, not unlike some of the comments journalists made following their 2010 experience.

"Graciousness is their default mode here. For the last two weeks, beaming has been a way of life. In a nod to the local vernacular, let me just say this is the nicest city I've ever been in."
— *The Los Angeles Times*

"You're gorgeous, baby, you're sophisticated, you live well…Vancouver is Manhattan with mountains. It's a liquid city, a tomorrow city, equal parts India, China, England, France and the Pacific Northwest. It's the cool North American sibling."
— *The New York Times*

"(Guests) will find the streets of Vancouver, a city of 2 million, so spotless, they'll think Mr. Clean is the mayor."
— *Miami Herald*

Tourism Vancouver's Promise is as relevant today as when it was first launched, particularly since guest expectations have evolved due to Vancouver's growing popularity and reputation since the Olympics.

Vancouver's Promise states: **The Vancouver experience will exceed guests' expectations. We will deliver superior value within a spectacular destination that is safe, exciting and welcoming to everyone.**

In order to support these tenets, Tourism Vancouver prioritized a number of initiatives and programs:

Exceed Expectations. Their Promise to exceed expectations involves delivering a product or service that stands out from everything anyone has experienced before, with guests recognized as the ultimate judges. Vancouver has won a number of awards that demonstrate adherence to this value, the most recent includes *Travel + Leisure's* 2012 "World's Best" award for the best city in Canada; *Outside* magazine's Travel Award for world's Best Weekend Escape (2012), and *Meetings + Incentive Travel* naming Tourism Vancouver one of Canada's top three Convention and Visitor Bureaus.

Superior Value. Providing superior value is not simply about cost. It's also about time and feelings – giving people what they want when they want it, and delivering an experience that is positive and memorable. To deliver on customer expectations, Tourism Vancouver encourages all Visitors Services staff to be certified through a province-wide World Host customer service training program. World Host was so successful during the Vancouver 2010 Olympic and Paralympic Winter Games that companies in London adopted the program so its tourism industry would be just as prepared for the London 2012 Summer Olympics.

Spectacular Destination. Delivering a spectacular destination is not only about physical beauty, it also involves maintaining a clean and sustainable environment for the enjoyment of guests and residents. Vancouver's natural setting is one of its greatest assets and it needs to be protected and preserved.

Tourism Vancouver is actively involved in helping the City of Vancouver achieve its goal of becoming the "World's Greenest City" by 2020. The organization recently hired a tourism energy specialist to work with its members to green their operations, helping to reduce energy consumption in order to save money and mitigate the industry's impact on the environment. This position is believed to be the first of its kind for a DMO and was implemented thanks to a partnership with BC Hydro, the province's power utility company.

Safety of Guests. Ensuring the safety of its guests is of paramount importance and one of the key factors tourists consider when they decide where to visit. Recognizing that safety is particularly important for travelers in today's travel environment, Tourism Vancouver expanded its Visitor Services program to include dozens of volunteers who roam the streets assisting tourists with directions and information in addition to creating an environment in which guests feel safe. Combined with the Downtown Vancouver Business Improvement Association's similar Ambassador Program, guests are almost always within shouting distance of assistance in the high traffic tourist and business areas of the city.

Exciting City. Vancouver is home to a wealth of festivals, sporting events, world-class attractions, arts and culture products, outdoor recreation and nightlife, all of which lend credence to its positioning as an exciting city. Attracting and supporting myriad entertainment options is an integral part of what attracts guests to the city and keeps them coming back. To promote and preserve the city's eclectic mix of attractions and entertainment, Tourism Vancouver launched the "Decade of Culture" in 2011. The initiative is part of the organization's goal to become a world city, and is designed to support, foster and grow the city's range of arts and culture offerings.

Accordingly, Tourism Vancouver works with numerous festivals and events throughout the year. One example is the Honda Celebration of Light annual fireworks competition, which attracts hundreds of thousands of guests to the city every summer. The organization also stages the city's most anticipated event for food lovers, Dine Out Vancouver Festival. Taking place over a 17-day period, the annual culinary promotion invites locals and guests alike to sample the three-course, prix-fixe dinners created by Vancouver's exceptional culinary talent, along with a range of complimentary food-centered events that enjoy sellout crowds each year. Recently celebrating its 10-year anniversary, Dine Out is now the largest restaurant festival in Canada.

Operating Tickets Tonight (Vancouver's only day-of half-price ticket outlet) also supports Tourism Vancouver's goal while driving economic return for the cultural community. Over its 10 years in operation, Tickets Tonight has established itself as the city's primary community box office, benefitting hundreds of producers and artists as well as locals and guests.

Another of Vancouver's goals is to become the world's most accessible major city — part of the destination's Promise to be welcoming to everyone, and a commitment that extends to people of every ethnic origin, religion and lifestyle. In the lead-up to the Paralympic Games, Tourism Vancouver and its partner DMOs combined to launch a program that assessed hundreds of hotels, restaurants and attractions to determine the level of accessibility for people with hearing, sight and mobility challenges. The assessments were also designed to offer to business owners suggestions for improvements to be more accessible to people with disabilities. The program has since morphed into a worldwide ratings initiative called Planat, developed by the Vancouver-based Rick Hansen Foundation.

Ultimately, building a brand means delivering on a Promise — and to become a premier travel destination, an entire tourism community needs to come together to fulfill that commitment. Travel is a great instigator; it educates, generates new ways of thinking and helps people shed cultural prejudice. Tourism Vancouver's responsibility is to help shape Vancouver into a model of urban civility, cultural diversity, environmental respect and compassion for the less fortunate members of society.

Rethinking the Future. Rather than resting on their laurels after staging the Games and opening one of the world's leading convention centers, leaders in Vancouver's tourism industry decided it was time for a thorough evaluation of where the industry was headed. The idea behind Rethink Vancouver was to carry out a year-long strategic assessment and visioning process that responded to two key questions:

▲ What is it that the tourism industry would like to accomplish in the coming decade?

▲ What does destination marketing for Vancouver look like from 2012 onward?

What ensued was a project unprecedented in both depth and scope. No other destination had conducted as extensive a stakeholder engagement process, much less a consultative process that was global both in terms of customer engagement and best practices peer review.

While Rethink was sponsored by Tourism Vancouver, the process was driven by the tourism industry. After Vancouver's tourism leaders and stakeholders worked together to develop a destination strategy, an industry strategy was developed with far-reaching implications for how they would work together in pursuit of these destination goals and how Tourism Vancouver would organize itself in the future.

Rethink is by no means conventional. It was a process of introspection, debate and discovery. While the outcomes of Rethink offer significant insights into how Vancouver can define the future of destination development, the entire process proved to be an enterprise that defined and found itself along the way.

Rethink began as a project with a deadline, and ended as the beginning of an ongoing quest. To date, Tourism Vancouver's Board of Directors has approved seven actions in response to the final Rethink report. These include:

▲ Develop a "World City" Vision, a collaborative process that comprises a broad community vision for Vancouver

▲ Commence with a Tourism Master Plan collaboration between Tourism Vancouver and the City of Vancouver

▲ Form the Lower Mainland Tourism Alliance, a joint initiative between Tourism Vancouver and appropriate partners

▲ Formalize Tourism Vancouver's role as a Destination Marketing and Management Organization (DMMO)

▲ Pursue a Network Organizational Model, for which Tourism Vancouver will explore a new approach towards engaging the tourism industry and stakeholders in building more business from key markets

▲ Develop a coalition with the Hotel Association of Vancouver

▲ Build Year-Round Activity through Events/Conferences, securing at least one major convention and one major event for each of the years from 2010 to 2012

Having hosted an event as complex as the Olympics, consistently delivering on its Promises and instigating Rethink have all given Vancouver a refreshed "can-do" spirit. Working closely with the tourism industry, Tourism Vancouver has reinforced its desire to invite the world to this special, world-class city, where hosts welcome guests with pride and where each guest is a guest of everyone who calls Vancouver home. ■

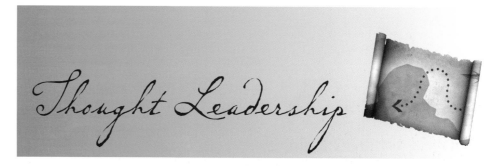

❏ The Brand Team considers all assessment information in developing a Promise. A Promise needs to address three fundamental questions:

- What should our destination's experience be?

- What distinguishes our destination's products and services from competitors?

- What is superior about the perceived value our destination offers guests?

❏ The Promise is written from the guests' point of view. It describes the expected emotional and functional benefits of experiencing the destination brand's products, accommodations and services.

❏ The Promise serves as the cornerstone for everything an organization does. It acts as a compass reading for everyone connected with the brand and also serves as a constant reality check to evaluate a destination brand's activities, performance and priorities.

❏ Service means nothing unless it's connected to how a brand wants its influencers, stakeholders and guests to feel.

❏ A Promise focuses on how an organization or individual wants its guests to feel, while missions or visions usually relate to what an organization expects to do.

❏ A Genuine Brand that has a real Promise should know how its guests and influencers feel every day and not have to wait for a rating service to determine its guest satisfaction.

❏ So-called branding initiatives that do not include a real Promise are a waste of time and money.

❏ The PromiseRule: Treat guests better than they expect to be treated.

Brand Blueprint

"Building on the Promise as a foundation, a destination develops the Brand Blueprint strategy to optimize its visual and emotional communications to become distinctive in the guests' minds."

Would you ever consider constructing a building, whether it is a simple one-story dwelling or a very complex skyscraper, without the aid of a blueprint? Of course not. Blueprints are drafted by skilled architects who are practitioners in the profession of creating, designing and planning all the necessary elements from which to build something, i.e., office buildings, libraries, homes, etc. In building or construction terms, certain styles or types are unmistakably identified as "architecture." Just as distinctive architectural styles set the tone or establish the nature of a building, so too are brands perceived by their architecture.

The foundation for the Brand Blueprint, every brand message and communication lies in the brand's Promise. When an organization utilizes our Brand Blueprint concept, it can expect to optimize the perceptions of its brand, thus advancing brand equity. Destinations need a prescribed technique for properly constructing and communicating their brand identity.

The Origins of Branding. Branding is not a new phenomenon. Craftsmen and manufacturers have long used marks of one sort or another to identify and distinguish their products from those of others, and examples of emblematic identification can be found throughout history. The earliest identity marks date back to prehistoric times, and even then the marks answered one or more of the same basic questions:

▲ Who made this?

▲ Who owns it?

▲ What is it?

▲ What makes it special?

The longevity and constancy of identity systems hint at the depth of the human need they fulfill. Marks on products have always indicated quality, craftsmanship and pride. In addition, brand marks provide an effective means of condensing and communicating a complex reality into a single, simple statement that transcends literacy, language and political boundaries.

Building a Genuine Destination Brand. A destination's personality and reputation for performance can distinguish it from the competition, engendering customer loyalty and growth. Truly successful destinations most often occupy unique positions in the consumer's mind's eye. A strong and motivating identity that guests know and trust can be elevated above price and feature competition. Successful destination brands can create higher occupancies, enhanced profit margins and greater certainty of future demand for their communities. To excel, a destination's brand image must be well-planned, nurtured, supported and vigilantly guarded.

Destinations that "live their brand" are ensuring that all messages, representations and innovations ring true to the governing Promise and strategy. The brand is the focal point of the destination's vision, the strategy against which all marketing and communication activities are gauged in order to maximize perceived value in guests' minds. It's all about strategy...not just execution.

In Bill Baker's book, *Destination Branding for Small Cities,* he quotes Malcolm Allen at Colliers International speaking to the importance of *Strategy.* "For me the key word is strategy, as in place, city or development brand strategy. I have often been struck by the power of major lasting brands to meet the changing needs of their customers whilst remaining true to their purpose and values – they provide a much needed (and proven) strategic guidance system."

The Brand Blueprint Methodology. The deliberate methodology for properly constructing, developing and communicating a brand's identity is crucial to maximizing brand equity. This is what we call the

Brand Blueprint. For a destination to be authentic and distinctive, it must communicate what the destination delivers, both in terms of its products and services, as well as in its attitude, culture and the way in which it communicates with guests.

A destination brand is forged from a multitude of components which, if crafted properly, creates an aura that is far greater in perceived size and value than the destination alone. A highly complex entity, a destination brand is not only the actual product and services, but also the complete set of perceived values, characteristics and attributes that differentiate it from other similar products and services. What is most important to grasp here is that a brand's identity exists primarily in the minds of the guests. When it comes to destination brands, perception is everything.

To position a brand for the future, it is necessary to first understand where it is today in the minds of the target audience. Building from a foundation of proper research is paramount. The Assessment we described in Chapter Three, including a situational analysis and environmental review, is necessary to reveal consumer attitudes, industry and competitive trends, and other relevant forces in the marketplace. From this secure footing, the Promise can be developed as outlined in Chapter Four, and the brand development cycle can advance to the blueprint process. The Promise is the foundation for the Brand Blueprint and every brand message and communication.

According to David R. Evans, CHME, Director of David R. Evans and Associates, the subject of a "brand" is one of the most misunderstood disciplines in organizations today. Taglines, slogans and logos are misunderstood and confused in many cases with the discipline of creating a strategy for a brand.

One of the best examples of a "one of kind" distinctive brand is Hallmark. Their long time tagline, "When you care enough to send the very best," was one of the best examples of a clear communication of their intended Promise.

This slogan was penned by a Hallmark executive in 1944 when they were trying to capture the essence of why Hallmark stood above the rest.

In today's electronic world where manners, common sense and a thank-you seem to have all but disappeared, receiving a card for any occasion distinguishes a person from the masses. If you care enough to take the time to buy and send a personalized card, you will make a difference in someone's life.

Strong brands gain authority and stature in consumers' minds by offering credible, coherent, attractive and consistent messages over time, from which consumers can form cohesive and meaningful patterns of association. Take Tiffany & Co. for example; everyone seems to recognize their signature Tiffany Blue™ color. What other brands can you think of that are known by a color alone, compared, say, to a symbol, name or slogan? The Tiffany shopping bag and gift box stand out in a crowd; they are instantly recognized and evoke a full range of emotional responses and images, from envy to sheer delight.

More than five decades ago, Walt Disney had an inspiration to not only open an amusement park but to create an overall experience that would make "dreams come true." When you enter one of Disney's resort parks, it is like entering a magical world where memories will be created and where you will have a unique experience. How did Disney imagine such an idea? His focus was always on creating the experience for guests first and product second: "The Happiest Place on Earth." The company is dedicated to its Promise that "Cast members turn the ordinary into the extraordinary."

To be recognized by guests as "authentic," a destination brand should signal what the destination delivers, both in terms of the experience and services, as well as in its attitude, its culture and the way it communicates with the customer. To be lasting, relevant and memorable in the minds of guests, the brand architecture must address and consider the prevailing cultural and business landscapes.

Many organizations today have considerable creative expertise within their management teams and hence don't have to look to outside advertising, graphic design or promotional assistance. Usually, the marketing department or division takes responsibility for the development of the blueprint and the associated visual communications and promotional executions.

The destination's Brand Team should determine the right internal and external expertise as appropriate to interpret the results of the Assessment and the destination's Promise to determine the blueprint.

The first step for this group is to agree on what are the most important brand signals which drive the essence of the Promise and how those signals should guide the creative process. The Brand Team's challenge, in partnership with the creative resources, is to identify a total of at least five signals (primary and secondary) to become guidelines for the brand's creative executions.

Once the Brand Team has developed a consensus on the brand signals, then it should begin the creative journey to develop the proposed executions. It should be clear from our discussion thus far that creative execution should not be developed until after the brand signals have been outlined.

There are five basic components of our Brand Blueprint. While traditional marketing practices would view these as five separate components, our Blueprint concept treats them as integral pieces which comprise one unit. As a total they should strike a harmonious balance resulting in creating a synergistic connection with guests. In this way, a Genuine Brand is perceived to have a larger presence than the destination. Utilizing the Brand Blueprint concept can optimize a destination's perception, thus advancing brand equity.

The Brand Blueprint consists of five basic components:

1. **Brand name.** A brand's name sets the tone for all future expressions. Great names resonate with guests, evoking memorable experiences.

2. **Graphic representations.** An icon, symbol or image that graphically depicts the brand's identity. Walt Disney's signature became the company's symbol. Starbucks has its siren and Target its red bull's-eye.

3. **Byline.** A descriptive word or phrase that tells consumers what a brand does or where to place the brand in their MIND'S EYE. An example would be "Visit" as in Visit Estes Park or for Ace, it's "hardware."

4. **Tagline.** The expressive phrase used to clarify or dramatize the destination brand's emotional and functional benefits to guests and potential guests. For example, "Super, Natural" for British Columbia or Nike's tagline is "Just Do It."

5. **Brand story.** Simply an explanation of how the destination came to be. The story serves as both inspiration and aspiration for stakeholders, guests and potential guests alike. It puts a face on a brand. The story brings the brand to life.

There is a fundamental difference between our Blueprint's philosophical approach and traditional marketing practices. In some cases, organizations believe that brand building is the sole function of the marketing department. We believe a brand's blueprint should be for the entire destination organization and not just one department.

Let's explore the characteristics of each component and see how they work together to ultimately position a brand in the consumer's mind.

A Brand's Name. A name is the first and perhaps greatest expression of a brand. It sets the tone for all future expressions, from a destination's identity to advertising. The genius of great naming is in the creation of a unique, ownable "sound symbol" that resonates in guests' minds and hearts. An effective name empowers the value-building process, strengthening the worth of the brand.

An effective name is the first signal a brand can use to create a distinctive, positive positioning impression. The science and art of name creation, however, can be a highly complex and technical undertaking. The process can include, among other things, the consideration of linguistics (language structure), sound symbolism (inherent meanings), acquired meaning (associations accumulated over time), intrinsic meaning (root word derivations), phonetics (speech sounds) and ethological (behavioral) considerations. Most important however, is that a name for a destination should be developed after the Promise!

In the destination world, organizations are moving away from bureaucratic names and adopting names that are more easily embraced by the public.

A Unique Graphic Representation. From spear-marking and petroglyphs to the sophisticated digital graphic identity systems of today, graphic design technology has been revolutionized. However, the fundamentals of identity design have not changed significantly. Contemporary brand identities speak on behalf of products, companies and destinations answering those same old questions and making qualitative value claims through a coordinated system of images:

▲ What is it?

▲ What makes it special?

▲ Who made this?

▲ Who owns it?

> A successful destination Brand Blueprint demands an unwavering commitment to its Promise, flawless execution and attention to the smallest detail.

The most visible symbols of a brand's strategy, trademarks and logos, encapsulate the complex personality of destinations into a lucid and concise declaration. With the capacity to convey big messages in a small space, trademarks and logos form the most international language in the world, which can readily deliver unequivocal and uniform messages to a destination's guests.

Trademarks and logos have become the calling cards that enable us to recognize products, services and organizations. In the case of destinations, they can provide guests with reassurance as to quality and origin, thereby permitting us to make reliable decisions when faced with many choices.

Logos and trademarks must carefully balance artistic goals with the effective interpretation, differentiation and communication of the real meaning of their brands. In other words, the question to consider is not how beautiful or creative a brand image might be, but whether it effectively and appropriately communicates the destination's Promise.

Criteria for developing an effective graphic representation include:

▲ Protectability – Consideration should be given to registering the mark as a trademark with the U.S. Patent and Trademark Office and in all other countries in which the brand will be marketed.

▲ Acceptability – Colors and shapes should be carefully considered to effectively cross cultural boundaries.

▲ Uniqueness – To minimize pre-existing associations, cut through complexity and ensure easy recall. Market research, including focus groups, surveys and interviews are helpful to determine guests' perceptions and association with a destination's mark.

▲ Compatibility – Graphic representations should work easily with other information likely to be in close proximity as well as strategic alliances with other brands.

▲ Flexibility – They should be able to translate into various media, including paper, digital and the internet.

▲ Recognizability – In key languages.

▲ Timelessness – They should be timeless in style and not get caught in current trends.

▲ Crispness – Graphic representation should be crisp across multiple mediums, i.e., digital, packaging, print, television, etc.

A Byline. Among marketers, advertisers and graphic designers, there is apparent confusion when the discussion turns toward distinguishing the relative differences between the use of a byline and a tagline. Bylines and taglines are definitely distinct, playing very unique and important roles in the total blueprint execution.

The byline should be a part of an organization's name or accompany the destination's brand name, usually below the brand name to clearly describe the business that the brand is in. This clearly communicates to guests and potential guests where to place the brand's products and services in their mind's eye. A byline is the descriptor of the brand.

Some marketing experts may argue that if a brand's name is very descriptive, then it does not need a byline. It's true that the more descriptive a name is, the easier it is for guests to position it in their mind's eye. The issue is to evaluate whether or not a descriptive brand name is enough by itself to communicate the brand's desired functional perception or what the brand does in a distinctive manner.

A Tagline. Taglines have traditionally been referred to and defined as "jingles" or slogans. In creating a harmonious architecture for a brand, the tagline plays a unique and distinct role. In contrast to the byline, a tagline is the expressive line used to clarify or dramatize the brand's emotional benefits to customers and potential customers. The tagline signals to guests how they hopefully will feel about the brand's experience.

Destinations want to communicate positive feelings to their guests and potential guests. Strong brand identities are created when these emotional benefits are communicated. Guests are concerned about how their experience will be, but they want to understand the practical or functional benefits as well. A new concept is to develop multiple taglines or theme lines for a destination. This allows for varied seasonal or activity messaging – however, always staying consistent with the spirit of the Promise.

Taglines can be used to help communicate your distinct point of difference from competitors. They can help cut through the clutter to reach out and attract potential guests to the destination, and in some instances, a tagline is utilized to reposition a destination. However, a tagline is not enough by itself to reposition a destination; it must have a new Promise and deliver its benefits if it expects to reposition the destination in the minds of its target audience.

A Brand Story. All Genuine Brands have a story, a legend about how they got started.

On the surface, these historical truths may not seem impressive. However, they really can be extremely powerful because they offer inspiration and optimism for a community. Preserving and enhancing a brand's heritage as it becomes more successful provides authenticity, inspiration and motivation for guests, employees and external relationships.

A brand's story puts a face on a brand, adds a personal touch and can bring a brand to life.

Summarized versions of a brand's story can be very effective in communicating a brand's essence. Everyone appreciates authenticity, and that's what a Genuine Brand is all about.

The Brand Blueprint. The five components are separate but whole, which is to say that no one component is more important than the others. As a total unit they should strike a harmony, a balance resulting in creating a synergistic connection with guests.

A well-conceived Brand Blueprint is all about design. Good design is the visual cue for everything the organization thinks, acts and communicates relative to its brand.

The blueprint's function is to communicate a consistent visual image that directs and consistently drives all the destination's communications and messages.

The Purpose is to:

▲ Consistently communicate the same visual destination brand.

▲ Ensure that everyone communicates the same message.

The Process includes:

▲ Creating a Blueprint creative brief that will set the tone for all future destination brand expressions.

▲ Developing a graphic representation that is the visual symbol of the destination identity, the iconic image or logo.

▲ Finalizing a byline which describes where the destination wants to reside in their guests' mind's eye.

To be recognized as authentic, a destination should signal the desired experience it delivers and its attitude.

Graphic Standards Manual. Most people who work in an organization, whether it be a for-profit business or a municipality, would never randomly change their organization's name without formal approval. For instance, an employee of a city named Big Mountain would never consider changing the city's name to Small Meadow on their own.

In today's world, there are so many communication mediums such as internal and external written correspondence, email, websites, printed brochures, faxes, business cards and digital media. This complex environment provides opportunities for employees to interpret and modify an organization's visual brand, i.e., its Brand Blueprint.

Sometimes, without even thinking, employees change the basic elements of their organization's brand such as its logo, font, size, color and the relative positioning of their brand's visual elements.

Hence, it is absolutely essential for a destination to provide every representative who uses or applies the destination's brand in any communication situation with a Graphic Standards Manual. A Graphic Standards Manual outlines the correct use of the organization's visual brand and approved variations for specific uses such as black and white instead of color.

In the absence of a Graphic Standards Manual, an organization may have many variations of its visual identity being used in various situations which depreciates the value of its brand and causes confusion.

The Life of a Genuine Brand. A fundamental measure of the success of a brand is its ability to be innovative, relevant and preferred over time. Brands have the potential for a very long life, provided, of course, that they receive regular maintenance, i.e., guarding against lapses of quality, counterfeiting, service obsolescence or an outdated image.

The best brands are potentially long-lived and robust. Though brand identity may require a minor remodeling from time-to-time, it should be done gently and carefully, just as Hampton Inn, Mercedes, Coca-Cola and other owners of meaningful brands have done over the years.

While some brands may wane because of shifting consumer needs or better competitors, others fall victim to derelict owners who neglect the necessary ongoing maintenance and investment.

These brands fade from consumers' consciousness and suffer the consequences in their financial performance.

A Genuine Brand requires a consistent commitment of time, attention and creative effort to continue to engage and maintain their desired position in guests' minds. In order to maintain the competitive edge and remain a leader, a destination must constantly protect its products, reputation and market position. In addition, the development of new products and services and creating exceptional, one of a kind experiences are essential for a brand's continued growth.

If you create the right Brand Blueprint for a destination, it's easier to achieve the desired brand perception. Genuine Brands serve as an emotional shortcut for a destination and its guests. The key is to make the destination a picture of the total experience in the mind's eye of current and potential guests. ■

Brand Insight

The Brand Blueprint Process at Colorado Springs

The Colorado Springs Convention & Visitors Bureau (CVB) understands the importance of having a true brand for a destination. In 2011, the organization created a budget item to go through a formal brand process for the region. As a result, the Community Branding Task Force was created to move to the next phase of brand development for Colorado Springs. The task force included seven city, county and community organizations in addition to the Colorado Springs Convention & Visitors Bureau (CVB). After a formal request for local proposal process, a local consulting firm was awarded the contract.

The extensive brand development process involved numerous research phases and workshops throughout the summer and fall of 2011 at a cost in excess of $100,000. More than 750 participants, ranging from business leaders, young professionals, residents, non-residents, guests, current and prospective businesses and historians, were recruited. The process included design workshops, interviews and quantitative research. The final result revealed a complete and actionable Colorado Springs regional brand strategy and various assets, including a Colorado Springs brand "essence" of alive, "truth": "Living Means Doing," tagline: "Live it Up" and designed logo.

The brand platform was created to serve as a benefit to the entire region. The brand speaks to guests, businesses and residents in a unique way, conveying a consistent message of what the area has to offer to each audience. All of these concepts as well as the logo were introduced to the community. After the reveal, the Community Branding Task Force's responsibility was, and continues to be, to facilitate brand implementation. This is done via three steps: introduction, information and infusion.

While the brand strategy was very well received, there was mixed community feedback on the logo design itself. After opening the lines of communication with the local creative community, the Branding Task Force announced a continuation of the collaborative process with the local community to design a new logo for the regional brand. It was also decided the result would be much more credible and widely accepted if a team of design, brand and marketing experts, separate from the Brand Task Force, oversaw the creative process. This new team was deemed the Curator Team. After an additional formal Request for Proposal process, the field was narrowed to four local design firms who each presented a visual brand reflective logo concept to the Curator Team.

After an in-depth, four-month redesign process, the new Colorado Springs logo was complete. With a unanimous recommendation from the Curator Team, the Community Branding Task Force approved the logo for use in promoting Colorado Springs to a variety of audiences, including travelers, businesses and residents. The new creative was launched in April 2012 with a multitude of positive feedback.

COLORADO SPRINGS

The Branding Task Force, Curator Team and small creative agency continued the dialog with the community to facilitate the adoption of the new Colorado Springs logo and strategy for the brand. Free decals were created and distributed to any community organization or individual who wanted to implement the elements into their own marketing activities. The leadership worked with multiple local platforms to continue to create awareness for the new brand and logo through TV spots, outdoor signage, bumper stickers, social media and other mediums. Organizations in the region were invited to various workshops informing them about the brand and how they were able to leverage it to achieve their own marketing goals. Success was reached when many of these organizations infused the brand into their messaging, promotions and communications in a way that makes sense for their objectives and audiences. ■

Thought Leadership

❏ Complete the components of the Brand Blueprint. First, identify and create the architectural building blocks for the brand's communication. Second, develop the brand's name, graphic representation, byline, tagline, brand story and messages. Third, ensure that all brand messages are consistent with "what the brand stands for" and the desired perceptions. At this time, the creative skills of graphic designers and advertising agencies can help bring your Genuine Brand and Promise to life.

❏ Brand Blueprints always follow the Promise. The essence of the Promise and the overall strategy for a destination drives the Brand Blueprint and the execution of its communications.

❏ Destinations should be developing multiple taglines or theme lines to provide optimum flexibility for seasonal or activity based messaging. Destinations should not have to be limited by one creative expression; however, all messaging must be consistent in reflecting the destination's Promise.

Notes

Brand Culturalization

"Bringing a destination brand to life."

When a destination organization aligns its mindset, culture and operations with its brand's principles and values, the Promise comes alive. For a Genuine Brand to be alive in the minds of community and guests, the organization must be internally focused on delivering the Promise through its structure, culture, reward programs, compensation packages and key activities. Words alone are not enough. Executives and representatives, at all levels, must be totally committed and demonstrate their commitment to the Promise through actions consistent with the organization's values. It is through sincere behavior that a Promise is reinforced among representatives and inspires them to accept the responsibility for delivering the Promise to their customers. Any destination organization can culturalize its Promise in a variety of ways to achieve optimum results. For example:

▲ Use internal communications to nurture morale and build esprit de corps, as well as commitment, through shared vision, mission, values and principles.

▲ Provide every representative with a thorough understanding of the Promise and expectations. Train everyone to understand how they can and how to adapt behavior to "live the Promise."

▲ Demonstrate how processes, practices and responsibilities are intrinsically linked to delivering the brand's Promise to guests, influencers and stakeholders.

▲ Change or modify policies to ensure that the DMO and the destination are consistently aligned with the Promise.

When brand representatives "buy in" to the fact that the Promise is genuine and that it is sincere and committed, they adjust their attitudes and behavior accordingly. The result is a greater degree of satisfaction among representatives, which leads to higher levels of guest retention and preference, which, in turn, leads to strong brand performance.

Bringing a Destination Brand to Life. For destinations and their stakeholders, the benefit of creating a truly Genuine Brand lies in its ability to attract new guests as well as build lasting guest relationships. Recognizing the value of brand power is one thing; doing something with it is quite something else entirely. The road map for destinations and constituents to live their Promise is Brand Culturalization. It is the process by which all representatives, both current and future, are exposed, indoctrinated and trained in the sum total of beliefs, behaviors and ways characteristic of a destination brand. This process raises the level of awareness with a view toward improving the ability – both individually and organizationally – to "live the Promise."

From the outset, it is wise to communicate to stakeholders, staff and board members that Genuine Brand creation is not simply an intellectual exercise. For many destinations, once they have performed the Assessment, completed the development of a Promise for their destination brand and obtained executive team, staff, board and community consensus, they think the hard work of creating a strategy for their destination brand is behind them. In truth, the real work is only just beginning. The greatest challenge – and most rewarding aspect of the project – is taking everything that has been created to date and making the destination's Promise literally come to life.

Genuine Destination Brand

"The internalized sum of all impressions received by guests and influencers resulting in a distinctive position in their mind's eye based on perceived emotional and functional benefits."

Far too many marketing plans are generic or similar in that they focus on product attributes and ignore an organization's culture. They do not take into account the totality of behavior, beliefs and attitudes that characterize the scope of all the associated organizations and people who comprise a destination. Some marketers think that simply slipping a Promise into a marketing plan or promotional message is the end game. A marketing plan must include practical programs and a detailed execution plan otherwise it is a fruitless endeavor.

Flawless execution of a destination's Promise makes a destination brand real in the mind's eye of guests. This is what "living the Promise" is all about.

Living a Brand's Promise. Living the brand requires a genuine belief and dedication to a disciplined approach for implementation; one that reflects the thoughts and actions of those charged with executing the plan on a daily basis.

How often has a guest been turned off, and consequently went elsewhere, simply because of the way someone handled a phone call, responded to an e-mail inquiry or didn't respond at all? Every guest interaction with a destination representative, at any destination touchpoint with one of the organizations that comprise the destination, can create a positive or negative perception.

It's important that everyone understands that there is an emotional and functional side to every interaction with a guest. Representatives must be emotionally capable of providing exceptional guest experiences in order to do their job well. Functional skills are important, however, they alone do not create a Genuine Brand.

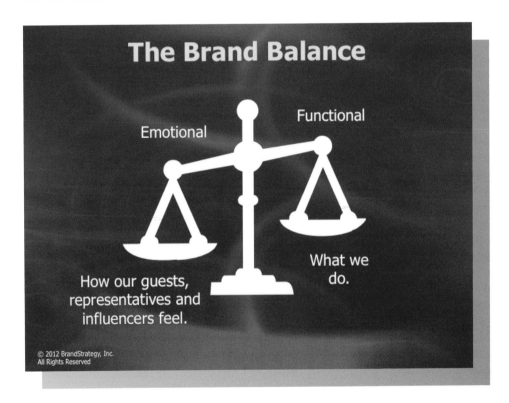

No matter how great a destination's brand and Promise look on paper, or how perfect a brand's positioning appears, or how creative the marketing and communication plan, a destination's reputation can be damaged – sometimes irreparably – by a guest's encounter with an indifferent or inadequately trained destination brand representative.

For a destination organization to keep faith with guests and "live its brand," it must align its internal and external brand ideals. This is what Brand Culturalization is designed to do.

A destination's goal during this step in the overall Doctrine Process is to establish the beliefs and behaviors – the way its representatives should conduct business and interact with guests on a daily basis. Destinations must ensure that everyone is aware of the "brand ways" and make sure that behavior-centric training is provided and reinforced to produce the desired brand perception.

After the Brand Team has agreed on the Promise and it has been reality-checked with various political and community constituent groups, it should prepare a formal presentation to the destination's board. The Brand Team's responsibility at this point is to capture all of the key elements of the Doctrine process thus far, including a culturalization plan. This presentation is designed to provide the board with an understanding of how the new strategy for the destination brand will impact the destination's overall marketing and operations.

The culturalization plan also incorporates the Brand Blueprint which is the architecture of the brand outlining the various messages – from visual, written to spoken – that will communicate the Promise.

To be recognized by guests as "authentic," the destination brand should signal what the destination delivers, both in terms of the experience and services, as well as in its attitude, its culture and the way it communicates with the customer. To be lasting, relevant and memorable in the minds of guests, a destination's communications and guest experiences must address and consider the prevailing cultural and business landscapes.

The chart below provides an overview of the Brand Culturalization process.

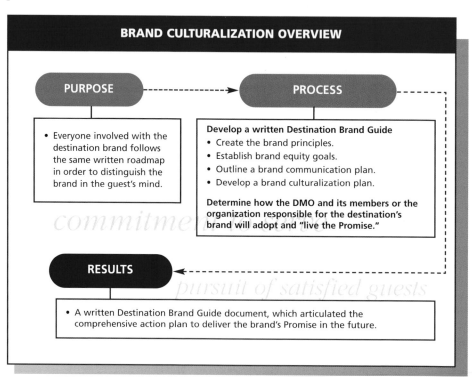

The Purpose of a Culturalization Plan. A Brand Culturalization plan is comprised of the actions and specific tactics that will literally create the personality of the brand. It is also defined as the process by which all representatives are exposed or subjected to the sum total of beliefs, behaviors and ways characteristic to a particular brand, thus raising the level of awareness with a view toward improving the ability, both individually and organizationally for a destination to "live its Promise."

> Living the brand is about delivering a distinctive or unique type of service or experience that enhances the guest's destination experience to the point where it is truly pleasurable and memorable.

Perhaps the most important trait of a Genuine Brand is its ability to create consistent perceptions based on guests' experiences. Consistent expectations are usually the result of a strong positive culture that exists within an organization. Therefore, the culturalization plan should define the correct culture and enhance its positive effect on each guest's experience. Now that the strategy has been created, creative agencies can really add value by crafting communication concepts that reinforce the Promise.

Everyone on the Same Page. Perhaps the biggest challenge is getting everyone in the destination, including representatives, volunteer leadership and members on the same page. With so many individuals in a destination focusing on different market segments, from travel writers and international tour operators to meeting professionals, there are often competing agendas and viewpoints from which to view the destination. In order for a Genuine Brand to succeed, it must do the following:

▲ Each and every representative of the destination must understand and adopt the Promise.

▲ Each representative must understand how the Promise can positively and relevantly impact their market segment.

▲ Each representative must emotionally invest in the Promise and understand the benefit it can provide to clients and guests.

▲ A destination organization's CEO must be a wholehearted champion of the Promise and commit to reinventing the personality of the community as well as its marketing programs.

▲ The destination needs to appoint a designated "brand steward;" someone internally who can monitor the daily activities of the destination, from its front desk operations to brochure design, so that the Promise is not compromised. While this is often not a full time dedicated position, it is often someone within a marketing function who can take the macro view of the organization's interests.

The chart below illustrates the framework for Brand Culturalization to occur throughout an entire destination organization.

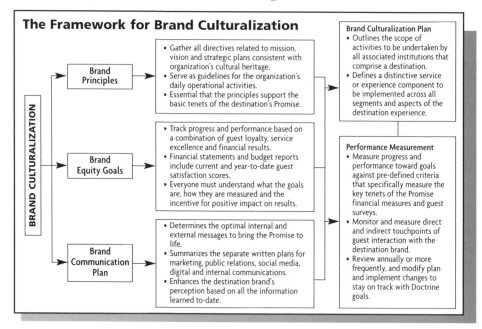

Brand Culturalization Checklist. It is obvious that each and every representative has an effect – positive or negative – on the guest experience. The first steps in creating a Brand Culturalization plan is for a destination to look at itself and see where the gap is between what is espoused in the Promise and how the destination undertakes it daily affairs.

Let's say the following imaginary destination has this Promise:

> *"Fantasy Beach is a lush tropical paradise with natural beauty, featuring residents who have a sincere interest in the well-being of their guests. Guests to the island leave feeling refreshed, reinvigorated and relaxed while enjoying a sophisticated travel experience."*

The key words in this Promise appear to be: Sincere interest/caring, beauty, refreshing and sophisticated.

If the Fantasy Beach destination adopts this Promise for its brand, it should ask themselves the following questions:

▲ How are phone calls and emails responded to? How fast is a request answered? Does their reception desk answer the phone in a friendly, caring way? What kind of feeling does the voice mail message communicate?

▲ What does the trade show booth look like? Does the layout and style reflect the Fantasy Beach brand?

▲ What is the organization's culture like? Are representatives stressed or refreshed and relaxed? Is there a perceived attitude of "caring" throughout the organization?

▲ What is the representative brand dress code? Is it relaxing or suit and tie?

▲ What is the office layout like? What are the pictures on the wall?

▲ How would you describe the events the destination hosts for clients, say in Chicago? Is the Fantasy Beach destination hosting a dinner in a windowless ballroom or in a restaurant that reflects the nature of the Fantasy Beach brand?

▲ What pictures are on the cover of brochures?

▲ What is Fantasy Beach's social media strategy?

▲ If Fantasy Beach is a membership bureau, does it host events and seminars in ways that say beauty, refreshing, sophisticated?

▲ Does the destination's communications of every type convey refreshment, beauty and caring?

▲ Is the destination's website consistent with the Promise? If the destination is selling relaxation and the navigation of the site is stressful and difficult, then the Promise is violated.

The bottom line is this: How do you want a guest, meeting professional, tour operator, travel writer or stakeholder to feel after interacting with the destination? Is the destination in alignment operationally and functionally with its Promise? A destination must first address its internal issues before it expects a community to embrace the changes needed to activate the Promise.

The Brand Culturalization approach is designed to ensure accurate delivery of a destination's Promise commitment and to enhance the level of understanding of the brand ultimately with everyone involved in delivering a destination's experience.

A Promise training guide is developed around the destination's Promise. This detailed guide is usually 10 to 15 pages in length and is designed as an instructional workbook which facilitates a highly interactive training discussion of about three hours.

> Guests must be able to trust the destination brand to deliver a distinctive, pleasurable and memorable experience each and every time they visit.

The culturalization plan is used as the basis to:

▲ Ensure that everyone understands a destination's guests', influencers' and stakeholders' desires, the Promise and the destination's critical goals and objectives.

▲ Establish a "how to act like a Genuine Brand" mindset for all representatives involved in a destination.

▲ Provide real solutions for actual day-to-day situations and improve job satisfaction.

▲ Inspire representatives to want to serve and deliver a destination's Promise to guests, influencers and other stakeholders.

▲ Engage and empower all representatives to excel in their work and create exceptionally positive experiences for guests and influencers.

Before a destination launches a culturalization effort within the community, it must first make absolutely sure that every representative, including those who work outside headquarters, such as sales offices, are fully versed and have a complete understanding of the Promise and why the destination is undertaking the effort. When stakeholders in the community learn of the destination's strategy for its destination brand, often they will ask a destination representative about the "program." The representatives need to enthusiastically embrace the power of the Promise and how it will enhance the destination's competitive edge. If a representative criticizes the Promise or doesn't understand its implications, that message will quickly spread throughout the community and undermine all the time, energy and hard work behind the strategy for the destination brand.

The destination's board is equally important in ensuring the success of the program. If an outside expert is used, it is suggested that he or she present to the board the complete findings of the Assessment, both good and bad, along with the conclusions and the discussions that have been shared with the Brand Team. A written Brand Guide that details all of the steps that the destination has undertaken, along with recommendations on Brand Culturalization which outlines the destination's specific strategy for its brand, should be discussed.

If there are board members who have served on your Brand Team, they should be acknowledged and given appropriate roles in the presentation. It is important for the board to understand that they are not approving an internal program, but launching a campaign that will involve the entire community, and ultimately it will be the community that makes or breaks the program, although, the destination will continue to play a significant leadership role.

Brand Guide. One of the great concepts for a destination brand initiative is to create and produce a Brand Guide. A Brand Guide can take many forms such as the *Enid Brand Book*.

Enid, Oklahoma recently completed a new brand initiative which included the development of the Enid Brand Book. This 28 page book outlines all of the key aspects of the new strategy for Enid's destination brand including Brand Introduction, Research and Planning, Brand Perceptions, Brand Attributes, Brand Essence and Brand Development and Delivery all packaged in a visually appealing guide.

Kevin Friesen, of Friesen Design, Inc. who successfully led the Enid community in their development of an entirely new brand, says that "at its core, a brand is the Promises that a product, service, company or community makes to its various target audiences. An effective strategy makes these Promises on purpose, so that every experience – every touchpoint – with the brand is delivered consistently."

"The ultimate goal," Friesen says, "is to build brand trust with your various target audiences. Brand trust is the feeling of security held by your target audiences in their interaction with the brand – that it will do what it promises it will do."

Berkeley Young of Young Strategies, Inc. provided the Enid Convention & Visitors Bureau with destination research and planning that led to the brand process and identified critical brand elements. Young says that "…A brand is also a personality that identifies a product, service, company or community and how it relates to key constituencies: customers, staff, partners, investors, etc. This includes psychological aspects – brand associations like thoughts, feelings, perceptions, images, experiences, beliefs, attitudes and so on that become linked to the brand from the experiential aspect."

"A purposeful brand image is a symbolic construct created within the minds of people, consisting of all the information and expectations associated with a product, service or the company(ies) providing them. It is represented through a name, slogan, symbol, style or design – as well as a combination of these elements."

A destination's brand is fundamental to its success. It takes a disciplined process to discover, establish and effectively deliver it.

Community Partnership. In the end, the Promise for a destination is all about creating pleasant, memorable and distinctive experiences. Remember, the guest may not always recall what you did for them, but they will remember how you made them feel. This is the essence of a Genuine Brand. But with so many seemingly disconnected elements throughout the community, how can the destination help a community deliver on this? Here are a few key ways.

▲ **Community Forums.** Rotary Clubs, Lions Clubs, schools, chamber of commerce luncheons and neighborhood groups are all excellent forums to communicate the destination's strategy once it has been finalized. The focus of this message should be that the Promise needs to be carried out and implemented, not by the destination organization alone, but by everyone in the community.

▲ **Civic Leadership.** As explained earlier, municipal and government officials should be involved in the development of the destination strategy. Presentations to city councils, county officials and other public groups should be scheduled to explain and interpret the brand initiative and the Promise. In an ideal situation, these leaders will adopt the brand as their own, and thus make it the foundation for future development and planning for the community.

▲ **Guest Services.** Does the destination have a Guest Information Center? How does it look? Where is it located? Is the staff adequately trained to "deliver the destination's Promise?" What is the atmosphere of the Guest Center? Is it utilitarian or welcoming? What messages, even if unspoken, does it convey to someone who is from out of town and seeing the community for the first time? Do they leave the center feeling better about the destination than when they arrived?

▲ **Airports.** While destination organizations may not have responsibility for operational control of its airport, they should have a strong alliance with airport management. Every airport should fully understand and embrace the Promise of the destination. When a guest first arrives at the airport, what do they feel? Do they feel welcomed? Is there a sense of arrival? If the airport is in a resort, are there elements that make the guest feel relaxed? Does the airport give a sense of what the guest came to the destination to experience? Is the airport staff trained to provide quality service and deliver the destination's Promise? Is the airport willing to work with respective security agencies to have security personnel undergo Promise training?

▲ **Front Line Employee Training.** One destination organization created a video that was directed at front line employees to teach them about the importance of the brand effort and how to deliver the destination's Promise. Companies throughout the destinations as well as hotels and other hospitality-related interests, were asked to show the video to employees when they were in training so they could incorporate these new skills. The destination's Promise is primarily delivered, not in the executive suite, but on the streets with everyday people. This program is critical to the success of the destination's brand initiative. One of the most important groups to address is taxi drivers, who are often the first point of contact for guests when they arrive in the community. One suggestion for components of this program is called G.U.E.S.T., an acronym for the way distinctive brands deliver on their Promise, each and every time they interact with guests, influencers and stakeholders.

> The destination brand comes alive through understanding, training and passionate perseverance to adhere to the brand's Promise consistently and enthusiastically.

▲ **Sales Training.** Hotels traditionally have taught their sales staff to sell brick and mortar and may not emphasize the destination. This has been changing as hotels and amenities are becoming more similar throughout the country. Additionally, with the advent of the Internet, price shopping is easier than ever. How do the hotels get leverage? By first selling the destination brand experience before the hotel sell. If a destination's Promise is well defined, unique and compelling enough, it will enhance a hotel's brand. After all, few people will want to travel to a hotel without thinking about the destination. Hotel sales representatives have to be on the front lines when it comes to the destination Promise and be unified and consistent about how they present the brand to their customers. It is recommended that formal brand training be developed that will instruct sales personnel not only on what the destination brand is, but how to sell the brand against the competition. The destination could partner with a local college or university in the community to develop the program and offer an experienced trainer who can go to the hotels to assist with this project.

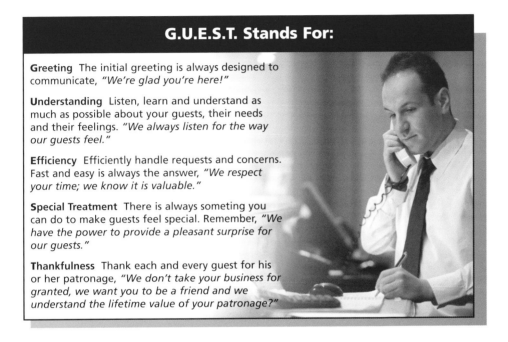

G.U.E.S.T. Stands For:

Greeting The initial greeting is always designed to communicate, *"We're glad you're here!"*

Understanding Listen, learn and understand as much as possible about your guests, their needs and their feelings. *"We always listen for the way our guests feel."*

Efficiency Efficiently handle requests and concerns. Fast and easy is always the answer, *"We respect your time; we know it is valuable."*

Special Treatment There is always someting you can do to make guests feel special. Remember, *"We have the power to provide a pleasant surprise for our guests."*

Thankfulness Thank each and every guest for his or her patronage, *"We don't take your business for granted, we want you to be a friend and we understand the lifetime value of your patronage?"*

▲ **Make it Magical.** Disney has a concept called "Make a Magical Moment" with guests. This could include a Disney character interacting with a guest, an unexpected surprise or something that delights the guest beyond their expectation. Disney encourages its employees to find opportunities throughout their day to do just that for guests at its parks and hotels. What can your community do to create magical moments for guests?

▲ **A Family of Brands.** It's all about partnership, as we will discuss in the next chapter, Brand Alliances. Many destinations are working together to create a regional Promise. Additionally, the destinations encourage each city to create its own addition to the official Promise that would complement the regional effort. This can also be done with other agencies in the community. Using the destination's Promise as a benchmark, a chamber of commerce or retail business association could develop their own addition to the Promise that would strengthen the overall community effort.

▲ **Events.** In 2003, the Memphis CVB launched its 50 Years of Rock 'N' Roll campaign, starting with a celebration at legendary Sun Studio where Elvis Presley recorded his first hit, "That's Alright Mama." While the campaign itself commemorated rock 'n' roll history, the trigger events and information all came from Memphis supporting its "Home of the Blues and Birthplace of Rock 'N' Roll" brand. In 2006, the 50 Years of Soul campaign, also originating out of Memphis, celebrated the history of Memphis Soul music and rhythm and blues.

President and CEO of the Memphis CVB, Kevin Kane, created the Memphis brand theme to market a single driver – music – to bring worldwide attention and visitors to Memphis. Because of his own passion and love for his hometown, Kane is interested in people and trends and all their backstories. Finding these special stories creates unique moments when landmarks or anniversaries can be celebrated and the brand stands out. The destination identity is enriched in a way that paid media or fabricated celebrations could never achieve.

Above all, a destination needs to assess the community and their current service delivery skill set. It is important for a community to develop its system of values that surround the destination brand, similar to the cultural aspects that characterize and define a people or country. Perhaps the most memorable Promise and culturalization program in the industry is Hawaii. The "Aloha" concept is defining, meaningful and memorable. While "Aloha" is indigenous to the island's culture, it is one of the best examples of compelling Brand Culturalization. The question is, who will be the next destination to create a culturalization program like the Hawaiian "Aloha?" ∎

Brand Insight

Seabourn: The Alchemy of an Attitude

Recruiting, Training and Managing to Be the Best. By the mid-1980s, the modern cruise industry had already begun its steep growth curve, with the entry-level mass market ships attracting lots of first-time, sun-and-fun cruise vacationers away from beach destinations and onto the decks. Premium brands like Holland America Line, Princess and Cunard were also actively cultivating a new audience of cruise travelers seeking world touring in a more refined style. The peak of the cruising pyramid was represented by Royal Viking Line, a Norwegian-owned brand that commanded the highest fares for passage to highly desirable destinations on its elegant, 32,000 GRT ships, which carried in the range of 600-700 guests. In 1986, Norwegian industrialist Atle Brynestad approached Warren S. Titus, the man behind the success of Royal Viking, with the idea for an entirely new style of cruising, operating from a new business model focused on an all-inclusive cruise product that lavished an unprecedented level of service on a smaller number of guests. Intrigued, Titus joined him in designing the first ultra-luxury cruise product, comprising guest accommodation in generously-sized, ocean-view suites, truly fine dining in an open-seating restaurant and the skilled attentions of a crew that numbered nearly as many as the guests. Unlike most cruise ships of the time, there would be only one class of service on board: top class. The fare one paid essentially purchased a period of membership in a floating private club, inclusive of all food and drink, including fine wines and spirits, Champagne and caviar. The staff would be hospitality professionals, recruited mainly from the top European hotel schools and reputable hostelries. They would then be trained, managed and well paid to provide the best service possible to each guest on every occasion, with no advantage to be gained from tipping, which was forbidden.

This philosophy of service was unique, and it gave rise to a culture that still prevails on Seabourn ships – a culture wherein every employee's intention and action is focused sharply on enhancing the guest experience, and on constantly working to anticipate, and then satisfy the guests' expectations and desires to the smallest detail. The hospitality staff was given an unprecedented level of autonomy to engage the guests. They were given permission, and even encouraged to add special, thoughtful touches that would personalize whatever service was being provided, and convey to the guest the server's understanding of, and concern for, their personal preferences. The goal was to go beyond merely satisfying expectations, to create "Seabourn Moments" that would surprise and delight the guests.

When Seabourn Pride was launched in 1988, named by then-Ambassador Shirley Temple Black, it created a new style of cruising that one discerning journalist noted as being "...in a class by itself."

Occupying, as it did, the most expensive niche in the leisure travel industry, Seabourn Pride and her later sister-ships attracted travelers quite used to luxurious accommodations, fine dining and skilled service. Nevertheless, the line's clientele quickly revealed a preference for traveling on the intimate, all-suite ship and voyages began to look like fond reunions as guests returned to sail with friends and familiar crew members with unprecedented regularity and frequency. So what was it that made these travelers, who basically could buy any leisure travel option in the world, suddenly so loyal to Seabourn?

The Seabourn model of hospitality is based on a constant signaling of recognition. Guests are addressed by name as soon as humanly possible, generally within 24 hours on the smaller ships. Service staff is expected to memorize names from a manifest and pictures as a part of their daily routine. This simple act of greeting guests by name (and always with a smile) initiates the surprise and delight response, and is the first indication to guests that they have entered a new dimension of personalized service. The crew is trained to observe and recall guest preferences – favorite drinks, how they take their tea, etc. This information is recorded and shared around the ship and across the fleet. That is the basic stuff of the onboard magic. But it goes beyond that, to a level of observation about the personal style of the guest. A waiter may serve one couple who are easygoing and jovial, like to joke with the waiter and be very familiar. The next table may hold a couple who are much more reserved and would be offended by much familiarity. The skill is to serve each guest in the style that he or she prefers, and it delineates the difference between rote "proper" service, and the sincere, engaged style that is Seabourn's hallmark. What this accomplishes is to put the guest at ease. Service that is not adapted to the guest's style can be slightly intimidating or off-putting. By contrast, when you realize that you are in the hands of a skilled professional who genuinely intends for you to have a great time, it is supremely relaxing. Guests may not be fully conscious of what is happening. They just know that they feel relaxed and well cared for, and that they don't have to worry about anything. Another positive result of this all-inclusive service is that it relaxes the relationship between the server and the guests. When a waiter on Seabourn asks whether you'd like something to drink, he is not trying to sell you something. He simply wants to know whether you'd like something to drink.

EXAMPLE: *A guest sits down in the Colonnade for breakfast, and the waiter comes over to the table and reverses his silverware, having previously observed that he is left-handed. The guest tells him that has*

*only happened to him once before (at The Inn at Little Washington)
and he's impressed. At lunch, in The Restaurant, as he settles into his
chair the waitress comes over, smiles, and reverses his silverware. Now
he is REALLY impressed. It becomes a game to the guest and his wife
to see whether it will happen at every meal, and it does, just enough to
keep them guessing.*

Another important feature of Seabourn as a destination is its uncanny
sociability. The ships are small, welcoming and unintimidating. It doesn't
take long to find one's way around and you are never very "lost." Public
rooms are scaled to encourage sociability, more like a social space than a
cathedral or a grand proscenium theater. Likewise the guest complement
on any cruise is a reasonably-sized pool or personalities in which
everyone is very likely to find people with whom they share attitudes and
interests. And yet it is also large enough that it is easy to gravitate away
from anyone with whom they do not care to spend time. Guests report
that the second-most important factor that brings them back to cruise with
Seabourn (Crew/Service is Number One) is "Like the people I meet on
board." They also like the ability to really get to know others, rather than
seeing them only rarely as often happens on larger ships. The
complimentary open bars and open-seating dining contribute to this
sociability. People can meet in the lounges and socialize with no
awkwardness about buying drinks or picking up tabs. And if guests meet
someone they like and wish to dine together, they can simply go to one
of the venues and the Maitre d' will seat them as they wish. Single people
traveling alone are routinely invited to join tables hosted by officers or
entertainers. (And no woman EVER crosses the restaurant floor except on
the arm of a waiter or Maitre d'). But invariably within a day or two the
guests themselves take over those duties, and unless they prefer it, singles
never have to dine alone, get "lost in the crowd," or have to be gathered
into mixing situations. In fact a substantial percentage of Seabourn guests
travel in groups of two or three couples who plan their travels together
from year to year. The net effect of this social pattern is a relaxed, club-
like atmosphere where conversation and socializing among the guests is
the dominant activity on board. There is very little of the organized
"mixer" types of activities that prevail on larger premium and
contemporary ships. Announcements over the public address system are
minimal, reserved generally for the captain's mid-day report at sea and
the announcements of ship customs and immigration clearances when in
ports. Enrichment lectures, classes and participatory games such as team
trivia quizzes are scheduled during time at sea, and published in a daily
onboard program, then guests are left to their own discretion about
attending them or not. Likewise after-dinner entertainment is aimed at
offering options, rather than trying to entice guests into one venue.

The science behind the magic of Seabourn's guest experience has its
own Periodic Table, in the form of the Twelve Points of Seabourn
Hospitality. This list of standards, which is carried on a pocket-sized card

by all employees, is designed to provide guidance for virtually any situation in which a staff member interacts with a guest. It has served for three decades as the true north of their service compass, offering a fixed point against which to set the course. Because it is to a certain extent exclusive and proprietary for Seabourn, I won't reproduce it here in its entirety. But here are a couple of examplary sections:

Never say "no." Offer alternatives if a request cannot be fulfilled.

If you receive a guest complaint, "own" that complaint and ensure guest satisfaction

Do not be afraid to make a mistake if you sincerely intend to do your job in a better way

...and number 12: Have fun!

And so what we find on Seabourn's ships is the synthesis of true hospitality. The staff members are professionals, proudly practicing at the highest levels of their trade. And those for whom service is a calling find it a stimulating and satisfying environment. They do, literally, have fun. And that is the attitude that guests perceive and enjoy. It is fun for them, too, to play their part in this exchange. They sense their importance in the equation, and they sense the staff's appreciation of their presence.

Out of the common stuff of human interaction, Seabourn renders gold by a subtle alchemy of attitude. ▪

❑ Prepare a formal presentation to the destination organization's board. The Brand Team's responsibility at this point is to capture all of the key elements of the Doctrine process thus far, including a culturalization plan. This presentation is designed to provide the board with an understanding of how the new strategy for the destination brand will impact the destination's overall marketing and operations.

❑ Appoint a designated "brand steward." This is someone in-house who can monitor the daily activities of the DMO as well as the entire destination, from guest services to digital design, so that the Promise is not compromised.

❑ Prepare and execute the Promise training guide which provides behavior-centric training for all destination representatives and stakeholders to deliver the Promise and produce the desired brand perceptions.

❑ Complete the written destination Brand Guide which outlines the comprehensive action plan for delivery of the Promise in the future.

Notes

Chapter Seven

Brand Advantage

"Strategic brand alliances enhance a destination brand's success."

Thanks to the continued growth of the digital market, the precedent-setting power of Internet travel marketing and an abundance of out-of-the-box thinking, more opportunities exist than ever before for establishing successful alliances.

Fiscal realities of the Great Recession have made tourism professionals creatively aggressive in their pursuit of lucrative alliances. In addition to generating increased market exposure, smart partnerships are flexible to quickly respond to last-minute opportunities, and have the potential to significantly reduce marketing costs or increase reach and effectiveness.

Online travel sites are loaded with partnership opportunities of all shapes and sizes. More than advertising space or rotating banner ads, digital cooperative packages include enhanced search engine optimizations, access to previously unreleased customer data and promotional links to other "equally-minded" sites.

This spirit of collaboration vs. competition is not limited to the Internet and has brought together many former competitors who have discovered that by working together as a unit, they are more effectively and efficiently reaching their targets. Hospitality companies, DMOs and even distilleries are capitalizing on the potential of alliances.

Successful Alliances. Brand Advantage benefits though strategic partnerships include:

▲ Extending the destination's reach into new guest markets

▲ Expanding the menu of opportunities for new and repeat guests

▲ Enhancing a specific aspect (hotel, restaurant, theme park, museum, historic districts, sporting events, arts and entertainment districts, etc.) or service attributes that heighten the overall guest experience

As we discussed in Chapter One, The "Bourbon Country" brand is a perfect example of brand alliances.

Guests are invited to explore Bourbon Country's rich tradition and proud history, and visit signature distilleries nestled among the beautiful scenery of the Bluegrass state. Distillers include well-known brands such as Wild Turkey, Maker's Mark and Jim Beam and the smaller, boutique distilleries include Barton 1792, Buffalo Trace and Heaven Hill.

More than $3 million has been invested in a comprehensive campaign to build The Bourbon Country brand. A coalition of regional tourism agencies cooperatively market Bourbon Country with a message of authentic culture, cuisine and lifestyle that resonates with regional, national and international audiences.

Collaborative agreements are nothing new for successful destinations. The hospitality industry has a long history of productive cooperative relationships, and Jonathan Tisch, chairman and CEO of Loews Hotels, authored a book on the subject, *The Power of We, Succeeding through Partnerships*, detailing that point.

InterContinental Hotels Group (IHG) has been providing world-class accommodations for world-weary travelers since its establishment in the 1940s as the hospitality division of Pan American Airlines. Today, the company has over 4,500 hotels with more than 650,000 guestrooms in over 100 countries and territories worldwide. The brand has long been respected for its commitment to outstanding service in its most remotely located properties.

To provide its loyal customer base with high-end properties where the company has no hotels, IHG established InterContinental® Alliance Resorts. The first Alliance partnership was created with the Las Vegas Sands Corporation, bringing their two high-profile properties, The Venetian Resort and Palazzo Resort, into the IHG marketing and distribution fold. The Scottsdale, AZ, Montelucia Resort & Spa also became a member of the InterContinental Alliance Resorts.

According to IHG promotional information, "These resorts enable you to experience these magnificent destinations while enjoying all the rewards of being an InterContinental guest...(they) are aligned with the spirit of InterContinental Hotels & Resorts and complement the InterContinental portfolio."

Alliance Guidelines. A strategic alliance is a serious business relationship built upon mutual trust, ideology and business opportunity. Alliances can occur without a merger, acquisition or other business asset combinations, and can be based simply on an agreement to leverage brand equity. However, conditions must be right for the alliance to succeed.

There are four criteria that should be evaluated prior to developing an alliance:

▲ The business cultures and ideologies of the organizations should philosophically be in-sync. They should share a similar dedication to quality and integrity along with having compatible reputations. Chances for a successful alliance is greater if their business cultures match and key executives "think alike."

▲ Destination management and partner companies must whole-heartedly support the concept and agree to meet regularly. These meetings indirectly represent a commitment to the success of the alliance and must be supported on all levels of the participating organizations.

▲ An alliance should never be viewed as a "short term" fix. Alliances should be viewed as a long-term investment which results in a competitive advantage for each brand. The results should be measurable, well understood by the parties involved and monitored regularly. Since the brands usually become preferred partners with each other, they should continue to seek ways to work together and strengthen the partnership's potential.

▲ An alliance must be approached as a relationship in the purest sense – like a marriage. As defined by *Random House Webster's Unabridged Dictionary*, a relationship is an "aspect or quality that connects two or more things or parts as being or belonging or working together or as being of the same kind...the state of being mutually or reciprocally interested." The goal is enhanced competitive advantage for each brand in its respective industry, whether it is a credit card or a destination.

Developing a Brand Alliance. Before establishing a Brand Alliance, a destination must first have its Promise in place and be clear about the destination's attributes and benefits of the partnership.

Here are a few questions to consider:

▲ What channels are most important to leverage the destination brand (media, stakeholders, financial, marketing, etc.)?

▲ What core competency does the destination brand bring to the party?

▲ Is the destination brand a real or perceived leader in a respective category (big city, culture, resort, beach, family fun, etc.)?

▲ Which brands are the market leaders (perceived or otherwise) in the category that the destination is looking to optimize?

▲ Are the operational and financial resources, technical expertise, logistics, etc., in place to best capitalize on the alliance relationship?

▲ Will the destination team have the time and resources necessary to further nurture the partnership beyond the outset?

▲ Are the destination's representatives receptive to working with other brands?

▲ Is there a specific brand that shares the destination's beliefs, values and goals or complements the destination's culture and management style?

▲ What are the risks involved in working with another brand? Will it alienate members in the community that have competing interests?

▲ Does the potential partner represent challenges that may alienate members of the DMO's board? These issues aren't often immediately obvious, and should be discussed well before the alliance discussions progress.

▲ Can the destination brand enter another category or "place" with the help of others?

▲ What are the destination's strengths and weaknesses? Is the destination aware of a brand that can improve and enhance a DMO's brand equity?

It is important to remember that a successful brand is based on both perception and reality and therefore must deliver on both. A creative Genuine Brand requires that as much importance is placed on the reality as on the Promise.

Alliances can potentially damage a destination brand if the proper thought is not given and agreements are undertaken lightly. If a destination or alliance partner violates the understanding of the agreement, it can cause long-lasting harm to both parties and hurt the destination's chances of developing further alliances in the future.

The key to a destination brand's success is a commitment to being distinctive. It is important for DMOs that are contemplating a Brand Alliance to determine the right fit, bringing together cultures, systems and resources of different brands to work together and trust each other to accomplish mutual goals and destination brand objectives.

Strong brands like Starbucks know that superior competitive market positions can be attained in partnership with established or new brands. Understanding the importance of keeping its brand fresh with new products and services, the techno-savvy company recently enhanced its popular mobile payment platform by establishing a unique partnership with Square, a company that is revolutionizing everyday transactions between buyers and sellers.

Square enables merchants of any size — from sole proprietors to national retailers — to accept credit cards. And by giving Starbucks' customers access to Square, these same users can access the local small businesses that also utilize the Square payment platform. According to Starbucks Chairman, President and CEO, Howard Schultz (Starbucks' press release — August 7, 2012), "We're excited and proud to accept payments with Square...Both Starbucks and Square take a similar approach when building products and running our businesses, and together we can bring the best possible payment experience to Starbucks customers." ■

Brand Insight

Individual Destinations + BestCities Global Alliance = International Success

The concepts of collaboration and strategic alliances are touted by business leaders, consultants and politicians.

An oft-quoted expert on this topic is Christopher Huxham, senior fellow at the UK-based Advanced Institute of Management Research. His popular definition of collaboration and alliances appeared in the *Journal of the Operational Research Society*, noting, "(collaborative alliances are) ...when something unusually creative is produced – perhaps an objective is met – which no organization could have produced on its own and when each organization, through the collaboration, is able to achieve its own objectives better than it could alone."

This descriptive formula of groups working together to accomplish greater goals is an excellent introduction for the BestCities Global Alliance. By bringing together high profile world-class cities, they as a group are better able to reach key meeting planners and site selectors to pitch and confirm future business.

An important key to a brand's success is its distinctiveness, and the BestCities Global Alliance is unique and requires its membership to maintain dozens of service standards which are regularly evaluated by a respected, impartial third party. By consistently anticipating and fulfilling the expectations of top tier convention planners, BestCities Global Alliance is also delivering on its Promise – the organization's commitment to excellence.

This assurance of quality is a powerful incentive for the meeting professionals whose successes are ultimately measured by the satisfaction of clients and their attendees.

Individual Destinations + BestCities Global Alliance = International Success. Around the globe, thousands of destinations are vying for a piece of the lucrative international congress (meetings) business. However, for associations, incentive groups and corporate conventions seeking unique venues for their large scale events, the exceptionality of a destination is not always reflected by the caliber of their respective destination marketing organizations.

BestCities Global Alliance was established in 2000 to address this challenge of service continuity. Recognized as "the world's first convention bureau alliance," the company proudly emphasizes its mission with a six-word tagline, "Best Practices. Best Meetings. BestCities."

The alliance provides continuous, professional attention and meeting services up to, and after events including bid support, guidance for visas, customs, arrivals and departures and assistance with local suppliers and contractors. This one-stop international meetings portal features leading destination marketing organizations utilizing each other's resources, promotional know-how and brand strength to their collective advantage.

The BestCities Global Alliance currently includes Berlin, Cape Town, Copenhagen, Dubai, Edinburgh, Houston, Melbourne, San Juan, Singapore and Vancouver. When promoted together, each of these unique cities gains an even stronger presence in the global marketplace.

Areas of Collaboration. The alliance focuses on four key areas to drive its business value:

▲ Service standards.

▲ An important point of differentiation for the BestCities Global Alliance is its commitment to consistently deliver high-quality services. More than 30 mandatory service standards have been implemented across the network and are regularly reviewed by the respected UK-based Lloyd's Register Quality Assurance (LRQA), a division of the 250 year-old Lloyd's Register Group. The company specializes in "assessing systems which are crucial to improving competitiveness." In this instance, these are specific actions utilized by destination marketing organizations. This level of verification provided by objective, third-party evaluations is unique in the convention bureau industry.

▲ The validation is working. In a BestCities Global Alliance survey of 200 meeting planners, exceptional ratings included customer service, quality of materials provided, overall experience of working with the respective DMOs and assistance with bid preparation.

▲ Martine Coutu, executive director, Société Internationale d'Urologie says, "The fact that our association has already held (or will hold) congresses in five of the members' cities led me to believe – and rightly so – that we appeared to be on the right track in our choice of destinations. One of the more valuable aspects of the BestCities alliance is their mission to establish industry standards and ensure that they are maintained, in order for clients to benefit from this certification of quality."

Client Relationship Building. Client workshops are regularly hosted by BestCities partner destinations, providing excellent "quality vs. quantity" exchanges with city representatives and prospective clients. The invitee database is the alliance's highly qualified, mutually-shared client lists.

In addition to highlighting the host city, these workshops allow for representatives from alliance destinations to network with the participating meeting professionals. At the BestCities workshop in Cape Town, 10 world/regional congress leads were generated with a potential economic value of US$39 million.

"Clearly, from the client's point of view, the BestCities client workshop in one of their venue cities is a remarkably beneficial way of introducing them and the Alliance personnel to the destination's available facilities," said Les Chappell, PhD, FSB, executive secretary, World Federation of Parasitologists. Therefore, the BestCities workshops act as an introduction to a potential venue and as a forum to exchange ideas and opinions. The infrastructure and organization of the workshop and the program are both exemplary and highly assuring for the client.

Knowledge Exchange. Alliance partners share tips and operational advice gleaned from previous and potential clients. The results are customized bid strategies better targeted to address specific needs of the groups. Meeting planners are the relieved and appreciative beneficiaries of this network, as their often complicated function requirements are quickly and accurately fulfilled.

Joint Marketing and Branding. The efforts of the BestCities Global Alliance are supported through www.bestcities.net, media releases and targeted advertising. Each partner highlights the BestCities brand identity in their marketing collateral, including business cards, e-mail signatures, letterhead, as well as websites and other electronic and print communications.

BestCities began its first brand assessment in June 2011, to establish a baseline of the alliance's brand strength and to better measure the effectiveness of future public relations and marketing efforts. As part of the assessment, meeting planners were asked to what extent a BestCities membership influenced their site selection decisions.

Results suggest that as a partner's brand is associated with BestCities, the destination receives stronger benefits in terms of client confidence and interest. Responses also confirm that clients have an appreciation of the quality standards required by the alliance.

Other frequent responses pointed to BestCities' global reach and uniqueness as a "one-stop-shop." Luca Segantini, executive director of the International Society of Nephrology said, "We completely trust the members of BestCities in terms of their ability to deliver profitable meetings, which benefit our entire membership. They work seamlessly together with our internal staff, and avoid the need for time-wasting bid processes and complex negotiations...their efficient model saves our time and resources and allows us to concentrate on the content of our meetings."

Future Growth. In 2000, the cities of Copenhagen, Cape Town, Edinburgh and Melbourne launched the BestCities Global Alliance. In 2003, Cape Town and Dubai became partners; 2005, San Juan and Singapore were added, and in 2012, Berlin and Houston joined the collection. Adding new cities to the alliance is crucial to BestCities' growth strategy. Expansion will include destinations in the USA (Chicago is in the preliminary stages of joining the Alliance), central and/or southern Europe, South America and northern and/or eastern Asia.

The overriding objective of expansion is to build a sustainable competitive advantage by sharing resource capability and leveraging the exceptional reputation of new partners and the cities they represent. This growth builds value for existing partners, gives new members access to benefits they could not achieve alone, and increases the impact of BestCities Global Alliance in the marketplace.

Potential BestCities destinations are evaluated on their profitability, and being a good fit from a corporate culture and relationship perspective. It is critical that new partners possess a supportive environment and have a solid track record of partnering, be accountable for results, practice open and honest communication and possess a flexible mind-set with long-term thinking. New partners are expected to commit to, and strive for, the highest service standards and shared business opportunities.

Alliance Advantage. BestCities Global Alliance presence in the market will:

▲ Enhance service standards within the convention bureau industry.

▲ Share business risk through additional financial contributions.

▲ Gain access to competencies that exist with new partners and transfer this knowledge across the alliance.

▲ Increase geographic and cultural appeal.

▲ Generate business opportunities with marketing leverage and qualified sales leads.

▲ The reach and impact of BestCities Global Alliance will strengthen exponentially as the advantageous benefits of collaborative destination partnerships continue to be realized. ■

Brand Index

For your convenience, we have provided the web addresses for the following list of selected brands that are referenced throughout this book.

It is my sincere desire that your journey through this book has been enlightening and inspiring.

A brand initiative provides an opportunity to evaluate your destination from every aspect, including how your guests, influencers and stakeholders interact with your destination and your organization. It's not just a marketing exercise; it is all about examining key guest touch points throughout your community.

Each destination that applies the principles of our Global Destination BrandScience further enhances this evolving science. As Joseph Marinelli, President of Visit Savannah explains, "I have been fortunate enough to use the principles of Destination BrandScience at two different DMOs. We often referred to the book when our Columbus (OH) CVB transformed into Experience Columbus. Later, when I came to the Savannah CVB, this organization used it as the basis in developing our brand architecture, Promise and mindset and ultimately led to our transition to Visit Savannah. Branding for the DMO industry has been undergoing a major overhaul over the last 10 years or so, and for good reason. Many of our products and messaging had turned stale. Having a tool like the new Global Destination BrandScience book will be valuable for destinations in understanding the necessary elements of building new strategies for a destination's brand, developing a Promise and communications to guests, customers, constituents and stakeholders."

One of the primary benefits of implementing the Destination BrandScience methodology is how it brings a community together to focus on its strategy. According to Peggy Campbell, President & CEO of Visit Estes Park, "The BrandScience methodology has brought our DMO and key community leaders to the table to define for the first time, a strategy for our destination brand. This community engagement is the cornerstone of our success, while also being a very enjoyable and rewarding experience."

Best wishes for your Genuine Brand success!

About the Author

Duane Knapp is recognized as the authority on building Genuine Brands and a pioneer in the field of BrandScience as well as in developing and implementing transformation strategies. He is Founder and Chairman of BrandStrategy, Inc., which has advised over 300 brands in 15 countries worldwide including corporations, communities, societies, professional associations, institutions, countries, world-class professionals, celebrities and successful individuals who desire to optimize their perception, image and success.

He has served on dozens of organizations' boards of directors, including Annika, Inc., American University in the Emirates, Federated Western Properties, Inc. and director emeritus of Longs Drug Stores (now CVS), and has held a variety of senior executive positions, including chief executive officer, president, executive vice president, vice president of corporate marketing, vice president corporate development and corporate strategist at public and private companies. These include Westin Hotels (Westin Enterprises and Discoveries retail stores and catalogs), Holiday Corporation (Holiday Inn and Holiday Clubs, Perkins Family Restaurants), The Promus Companies (Embassy Suites, Residence Inn, Hampton Inn, Homewood Suites and Harrah's Casinos) and Cinnabon World Famous Cinnamon Rolls. He advises leading law firms relating to high-profile brand and intellectual property matters and has specific expertise in the fields of travel and hospitality, food and beverage products, restaurants, retailing, health care, financial services and real estate development. He has been approved as a Senior Gaming Officer by both the New Jersey and Las Vegas Gaming Authorities.

Mr. Knapp has taught and lectured widely at universities and graduate schools throughout the United States, including Vanderbilt, Stanford, the University of California, the University of Colorado at Boulder and Seattle University. Mr. Knapp is the leading keynote speaker on the subject of building Genuine Brands. He has been published, quoted or featured in hundreds of publications, including *BusinessWeek, Brandweek, CFO Magazine, Association Management, Marketing, Washington CEO, Bankers Magazine, Design Forum, Focus Magazine, Risk Management, Forbes Magazine Travel, Distribution Reports, Private Clubs Magazine, Fortune Magazine* and *International Journal of Medical Marketing,* as well as *The Seattle Times, The Journal of Commerce* and many private corporate and association publications as well as television and radio talk shows.

He is the author of several books including ***Global Destination BrandScience***™. The ***BrandPromise***® was published by McGraw Hill as well as the ***BrandMindset***®. The ***BrandMindset*** book was selected by IBM and American Express as the "must read" book for their top 400 executives. It is available in seven languages and is considered the definitive guide to building Genuine Brands. He is also the co-author of ***Destination BrandScience***™, published by the Destination Marketing Association International.

Duane Knapp's ***BrandPromise*** philosophy is highly acclaimed and has been extensively referenced and quoted in many books and publications, including Tim Sanders' bestseller, *Love is the Killer App*, Nick Wreden's *FusionBranding*, Michael Levine in *A Branded World*, David Aaker's, *Building Strong Brands* and Tony Simons, *The Integrity Dividend*. Knapp also wrote the foreword for *License to Serve*.

Mr. Knapp earned his BA in Business Administration from Western Michigan University and his MBA from the University of Toledo. He also completed a postgraduate program in Strategic Marketing at the Stanford University Graduate School of Business.